Streams

Of

Joy

Devotions of God's Goodness
From the authors of Winged Publications

Copyright © **2018**

Written by: Winged Publications authors

Published by: Winged Publications

ISBN-13: 978-1-947523-13-5
ISBN-10: 1-947523-13-9

DEDICATION

To all those who desire to find joy in their life!

TABLE OF CONTENTS

A Hole in the Fence

By Sherri Stewart

*I lift my eyes to the mountain; where does my help
come from? Psalm 121:1*

One of my favorite verses is part of a psalm of ascent. Songs of ascent were sung by the Israelites as they made their pilgrimage to Jerusalem for holy days. It wasn't an easy journey because the mountains held hidden dangers—thieves ready to pounce, steep places difficult to navigate in the dark, and wild animals lurking in caves. That is why the psalmist said, "I lift my eyes to the mountain; where does my help come from? My help comes from the Lord, the Maker of heaven and earth." The Psalmist was afraid, indeed, but he reminded himself that His Lord, who made that mountain, could keep his foot from slipping.

I've been in some mountaintop situations; not the ones where I feel triumphant and wonderful. No, the ones where I trembled with fear because the elements were terrifying. Those were the times I cried out for God's help by quoting verses as the psalmist did.

I remember Kay Arthur telling about a lady in Chattanooga who had just attended her first Bible study and learned about the value of memorizing scripture. As she stopped at a red light, a man jumped into her car, put a gun to her head, and said, "Drive, lady." Scared to death, she remembered something she heard at the bible study; something about speaking scripture out loud when the situation warranted it. Problem was—her memory wasn't so good. All she could remember about the verse was it had something to do with being safe under the wings of a chicken.

The words poured out, "Chicken, chicken, chicken." The guy looked at her and said, "You're crazy, lady, let me out."

The lesson: The Word of God works, even when quoting wrong. I remember back when I used to run, I was jogging around the periphery of my subdivision in Calgary, Alberta. It was early—5:30 in the morning, but the sun was coming up. From as far as my eye could see there was nothing but prairie grass. As I rounded a curve, a car slowed down beside me. I was on the sidewalk, but the car was maintaining the same speed I was running, and I was slow. Nothing good could come from this situation. Not a human in sight, not a car in sight, no house to run to.

Then I remembered Elisha. He'd prayed that his servant could see the angels that protected them from the approaching enemy in II Kings 6:17-20. So that's what I prayed. "God, could you send me angels to protect me…now?"

As I ran, the privacy fence on my right side was taller than I, but out of nowhere, a hole appeared in the fence—a me-sized hole, and I'm not petite. I thanked God, climbed through the hole, and ran through someone's backyard.

Think about it. Who has a human-size hole in their backyard fence? I didn't even quote a verse; I summarized a fractured version of a bible story. But God opened up that hole.

Lord, thank you for your protection when we

confront the mountains in our lives with all their hidden dangers. And thank you for providing protection when the enemy approaches. Even when we come to you with misquoted verses and quick requests for help, you're there ready to take care of your children. We have the best father. In Jesus' name, Amen.

A Different Kind of Handsome

By Sherri Stewart

"The LORD does not look at the things people look at.
People look at the outward appearance, but the LORD
looks at the heart."
I Samuel 16:7

As I reflected on one of the lessons my main character deals with, I realized that some of my other books feature the same lesson. Simply put, Nicole, a flight attendant, judges a man based on outward appearance. How superficial, I thought. Don't most people overcome that in their teenage years?

In two other books, the female characters make assumptions about the male leads based on their outward appearances. Of course, looks are deceiving, and the men's inner strength, compassion, and convictions win the women over. Nothing original here. Turn on any Hallmark movie, lower the volume, and just by looking at the male characters, you can predict that the guy with stubble growing on his face will be the hero of the story, while the man in the Brook Brothers suit will make an involuntary exit.

So why did I choose that lesson to feature in my books? I didn't; it chose me because I've judged others based on outward appearances. I'm a starer. You won't find that word in the dictionary, but it describes a person who, like me, watches people. For some reason, starers believe that others won't notice that they're staring at them. But sometimes, they do. Then we starers glance away and look for the nearest exit. I've read that writers are great observers of life around them. I like that—it puts a better spin on the act of staring.

I married a scruffy-looking guy. We met in a diner. I taught French in a high school full time during the day but couldn't make ends meet without working a night job.

The first time I saw him I wasn't impressed. He sat on a stool at the counter and showed me how to make a proper cup of tea. Not the kind where you float a teabag in a cup of hot water, but the kind where you steep the tea in a pot. He worked for a hockey team. I wasn't impressed. I'd never liked hockey.

Then he asked me out, but not only that, but he told me I could pick any restaurant. I was in hog heaven. Imagine choosing a restaurant in Atlanta, Georgia, when your diet consists of different flavors of Ramen Noodles. Bill Gates and Apple hadn't been born yet, so I conferred with friends, students, faculty members, and finally chose Anthony's—an Antebellum restaurant—très chic! Two years later, we had our wedding reception there.

It takes time to fall for a scruffy-looking guy. His clothes needed pressing and his car smelled like a locker room. It came by the smell honestly—the backseat was full of hockey skates. But I noticed things about him— the way he searched for a watering can for a Russian defenseman who was having trouble growing a houseplant. Or the way he always brought me back a candy bar or a keychain from whatever city they were playing in.

I learned to love hockey—I've been to over a thousand games—and we've been married for forty years. He still doesn't care about a crease in his pants, and he leaves crumbs on the table, but my husband is a kind, thoughtful, sensitive, trustworthy, gentle, loving man.

Appearance can get in the way of sound judgment. In I Samuel 16:7, God warned Samuel about Saul. "Do not consider his appearance or his height, for I have rejected him. The LORD does not look at the things people look at. People look at the outward appearance, but the LORD looks at the heart." I'm so glad I wasn't deceived by the polished, debonair Patricks of my youth, but gave the scruffy guy a second glance.

Dear Lord, I am so glad you are not human. Your logic is the exact opposite of the logic of man. We posture and network to be noticed, to be chosen first. You say the last shall be first. We favor attractiveness, smarts, riches, and power. You favor the humble, the poor, the meek, the servant. Help us to be more like you, to desire the same traits in our friends, not just because we want to please you but because you change our hearts to such an extent that we actually favor the same things you do. In Jesus' name, amen.

Sherri Stewart

Social Media Contacts
Amazon Author Page
https://www.amazon.com/author/sherristewart/

Email sherristewart2@yahoo.com

Website www.stewartwriting.com/blog

Facebook
https://www.facebook.com/sherristewartauthor/

Twitter https://twitter.com/machere

Goodreads
https://www.goodreads.com/author/show/758893.S
herri_Stewart/blog

Jasmine Blooming Tea

By Anita Higman

The experience of watching a blooming flower tea ball open in your cup is not to be missed, especially if you are a lover of fine teas. I witnessed this wonderment in an historical movie, and knew I had to experience this enchantment for myself. I found a jasmine version of the tea, and these hand-sewn tealeaves did indeed open in the hot water to reveal a hidden flower inside. The sweetness of the jasmine along with the blooming effects made it a fairytale-like encounter in my cup. There was only one disappointment. The ball didn't open nearly as fast as I thought it would. I had to sit still and be patient for the full blossoming magic to take place.

Isn't this just like our impatience with God when it comes to our spiritual journeys? We want our spirits to be bursting with God's knowledge and wisdom and faith. Right now. This very minute. When in truth, this "being still" will take years—a lifetime, really, to wholly mature so that people can taste our sweetness, witness the wonderment, and experience the full blooming effects of His nurturing within our souls.

We are bound to thank God always for you, brethren, as it is meet, because that your faith groweth exceedingly, and the charity of every one of you all toward each other aboundeth. 2 Thessalonians 1:3 (KJV)

Chocolate Tea

I am a big tea fan and a lover of chocolate, but when I discovered "chocolate tea" I have to admit my smile sort of twisted out of shape. Well, hey, I'm either in the mood for tea, or I have a craving for chocolate. We humans—even our taste buds—have a way of compartmentalizing our lives.

I'm sure in my spiritual journey I've done a similar but more profound version of that same partitioning. I keep God near when I'm in the mood for his healing touch, his blessings, his tender mercies in my life, but when any of the goodies are connected to a growth experience that might be painful or when he's showing me a transgression that requires nothing less than repentance and change, my smile gets twisted again. It's hard for me to mingle and enjoy those two attributes of God, even though they are both very good. I remind myself that His ways are not my ways and that He loves me enough to keep me ever growing in His grace.

We don't need to endure the blending of two dissimilar culinary flavors such as tea and chocolate, but we need to drink deeply of all of God's gifts and desires for us. It's the only way to taste real joy and to savor lasting peace. Cheers!

Every branch in me that beareth not fruit he taketh away: and every branch that beareth fruit, he purgeth it, that it may bring forth more fruit. John 15:2 (KJV)

Lord, may I always embrace all that You have for my life, whatever it may be. Amen.

www.anitahigman.com

CBA bestselling and award-winning author, Anita Higman, has forty-five books published and has been honored in the past as a Barnes & Noble "Author of the Month" for Houston.

Anita Higman has a BA degree in the combined fields of speech communication, psychology, and art from Southern Nazarene University, and she is a member of American Christian Fiction Writers. Anita has been featured on The Harvest Show, a Christian program with eight million regular viewers, Disney Radio, and Houston's TBN and PBS.

A Masterpiece in the Making

by Alexis A. Goring

"God takes the **broken** pieces that Satan leaves behind and makes MASTERPIECES." – Pastor Pranitha Fielder

"For we are God's masterpiece. He has created us anew in Christ Jesus, so we can do the good things he planned for us long ago."
– Ephesians 2:10 (NLT)

Shattered. Broken. Devastated.

We've all been there or will be there at one point in our lifetime. If you manage to go through life without ever experiencing pain then that is not normal. Just like a character said in the movie "The Shack", if you're looking for a pain-free life, you're not going to find one.

We live in a pain-filled world because it is a sin-filled world, which results in pain, heartbreak, devastation and despair entering our life stories.

No one escapes this life on Earth without some form of pain. It happens to you at least once in your lifetime— whether it is a broken arm or a broken heart, you *will* experience pain.

So when you experience pain, what can you do? You can turn to your Creator (God) and ask Him to help you get through the tough times. He can soothe your broken mind, repair your heart, and restore your life. If it's a physical or emotional pain, He can work through others for your benefit. People like counselors, doctors, first responders, physical therapists, etc. are here on Earth to help you heal.

Recently, I was talking to someone and they told me that nobody's perfect, we all have something to work on. Before she could continue speaking, the title of this devotional "A Masterpiece in the Making" downloaded into my mind and I had to end the phone conversation immediately and start writing this devotional because I realized that God just downloaded inspiration to my brain and He never wants me to keep His messages to myself. So here I am, writing this message to you in hope of encouraging your heart!

I titled this devotional "A Masterpiece in the Making" because if you are a human on planet Earth and you've decided to follow Jesus Christ then you my dear friend, *are* a *masterpiece in the making*!

I want to encourage you to not give up when pain or problems enter your life. But instead, turn to God. He is in control and He will help you.

Did you know that God truly believes that *you* are His *masterpiece*? He clearly states that truth in the Bible. Here's the verse in Ephesians 2:10 (NLT): "For we are God's masterpiece. He has created us anew in Christ Jesus, so we can do the good things he planned for us long ago."

So now that you know that *you* are God's special creation, His masterpiece, embrace this truth and be encouraged! God will never ever leave you. He loves you too much to leave you broken, shattered and devastated. He only wants to lift you up and save your soul. He loves you with *all* of His divine heart!

If you're a perfectionist like me, then you may worry over things or situations in your life that are far from perfect. I'm here to tell you today to let go and let God. Trust Him to work with you on the areas in your life that need improvement. Trust Him to work it all together for your good (Romans 8:28). Allow God to make you into the original masterpiece that He knew you were before you even were aware of it. God knows how to look at rubble and see a diamond. But He does more than see your potential; He helps you to grow into it, which is why all who follow Christ are a masterpiece in the making!

Remember, when God starts making a masterpiece, he carries it to completion just like He promises in Philippians 1:6.

I hope that you are encouraged by this devotional. May God bless your dear heart! Always remember that He loves you and He will never leave you (Hebrews 13:5) and that *you*, my dear friend, are His masterpiece!

Let's Pray: Dear God, Help me to remember that I am your masterpiece, created to do good works during my time on planet Earth. Thank You for making me and shining through my brokenness. Help me to fulfill Your purpose for my life story. In Jesus' Name I pray, Amen.

Before I Call

By Alexis A. Goring

"Before they call I will answer; while they are still speaking I will hear."
~Isaiah 65:24 (NIV)

One day, God answered a prayer that I did not pray. His providence amazes me! Allow me to tell you the story of the time when God answered me before I called.

It was an ordinary weekend. The food supply in the house was low, but I didn't have money to buy groceries. I found myself thinking, *I wish I had money to go to Panera, but I need to save my money to pay bills.* So I determined to do without. I stayed home and went about my business.

A few hours later, I was talking to a writer friend who I was helping by providing feedback on certain elements in her story. She told me that she appreciated my time and talent, so she wanted to give me a gift as a thank you for my pro bono services. She asked me to choose what I wanted and suggested options like gift cards from Amazon and Starbucks. My first thought was about my wish list of books on Amazon, so I asked for an Amazon.com gift card. So she sent that to me via e-mail within the hour.

But since our arrangement was ongoing, she'd offered to send more than one gift throughout the editorial process. And I decided, since I was craving Panera, that's what I'd ask for. But I wondered, *how*? I didn't know if Panera had e-cards. So I called a local restaurant, and they directed me to their company website where indeed there was an option to send e-gift cards. I copied the direct link and sent it to my writer friend who then agreed that my payments going forward would be e-gift cards to Panera!

After our conversation, I realized God had answered me before I called. I never stopped and prayed to Him to make a way for me to have enough extra money to go to Panera, I simply thought it and pushed the thought aside when I realized it wasn't happening right now. But God heard my thoughts, and He decided to bless me unexpectedly!

God is so good. He watches over all of His children—the ones who know Him and the ones who do not know Him *yet*. He wants us *all* to be saved in His Kingdom, to make it to Heaven and spend eternity in His presence. But we have to choose to accept the gift of salvation that He offers through His Son Jesus Christ, and we have to choose to follow Him.

Falling in love with Jesus and following Him have been the best decisions I've made in my life. I wouldn't be able to stand through the trials and storms of life without Him and His provision. Just like God provided for me by answering my prayer before I asked, He wants to provide for you too.

The Bible says that He takes care of the sparrows in the sky, and we (His children) are worth far more than sparrows, so He will definitely take care of us. My story of how God provided for me is just a small picture of the grand scheme of things that God does for His children.

God is always at work in our lives. Even when we

cannot see Him or feel His presence, He's still there. The Bible says in Hebrews 13:5 that God will *never* leave or forsake us. It's a promise from His heart to ours, and God faithfully keeps *all* of His promises!

I'm still growing in my faith walk with God, and I love it when He reminds me of Bible verses that apply to my experience. The Bible verse that speaks to my recent experience involving my desire for Panera reminds me of Isaiah 65:24 (NIV) in which God says, "Before they call I will answer; while they are still speaking I will hear."

It delights my soul that God taught me a lesson of His providence through answering my unspoken prayer regarding my desire for food from Panera. He used this to remind me that He cares about every detail as big as paying a mortgage to as small as buying a favorite meal from your favorite café.

So I'd like to encourage you to go to God first with your every concern, request, and praise report. Then trust Him to provide for your every need… and sometimes your wants too! Trust that sometimes, even before you go to Him in prayer, He'll hear you and answer your heart's desire in a totally unexpected way like He did for me. Why? Because before we call, God will answer; while we are yet speaking, God will hear!

Let's Pray: **Dear God, You are amazing! Thank You for all that you do for me. I love that you answer my prayers before I call. You care about every detail of my life. Please help me to daily experience Your blessings, Your providence and Your peace. In Jesus' Name I pray, Amen.**

God's Waiting Room

A devotional by Alexis A. Goring

"Even the youths shall faint and be weary, and the young men shall utterly fall, but those who wait on the Lord shall renew their strength; They shall mount up with wings like eagles, they shall run and not be weary, they shall walk and not faint." – Isaiah 40:30-31 (NKJV)

I've been waiting for my creative career dreams to come true for some time now and lately I realize that God has me in what I like to call "God's Waiting Room". No, it's not a physical waiting room located in a hospital. It is more of a spiritual one where I'm waiting on my dreams to come true.

These last several years have been filled with highs and lows. After being laid-off from my last day job, I have not been hired by a new boss. So thinking that maybe I need to be my own boss, I started my own business (an editorial service). The clients that I've had are happy with my work but I don't have enough clients to make a solid living financially, which is why I've been applying for another day job. However, the rejection letters keep rolling in. I've told some of my author friends that I've received more rejection letters from potential employers than I have from literary agents.

Recently, I was sinking into despair but then in the midst of my worrying, God encouraged my heart when He led me to this song by Lincoln Brewster called "While I Wait." The song is essentially about waiting on the Lord and trusting Him with the outcome.

It's also about trusting God in the process as you wait on Him to take you to where He wants you to be in life. This song taught me a few very important life lessons. Allow me to explain the lessons I'm learning while seated in God's Waiting Room.

If you're a human on planet Earth, you will have seasons of waiting. It varies from person to person. Some are waiting to graduate from school and enter the workforce. Some are waiting to marry their soul mate. Some newlyweds are waiting to purchase or build their dream home. Some married couples are waiting on a baby of their own. Some professionals are waiting on the job of their dreams. Some are waiting on peace to prevail in their land. Some are waiting on God to answer their prayers. We're all waiting on something or someone. While you're waiting, I want to encourage you to listen to this song ("While I Wait" by Lincoln Brewster).

Here's what I've learned from the song and from my own experience of being in God's Waiting Room: Though I don't have the answers, I will trust God all the same. In his song "While I Wait", Lincoln Brewster says that sometimes miracles take time. I'm determined to worship God while I wait and will continue trusting Him. He makes miracles every day. It's only a matter of time before He makes one for me. I know this because God is faithful *every day*. His promises are permanent and He is faithful to fulfill each one. I don't understand the wait but I know that God is with me. I do not have all the answers but I serve a God who is sovereign, faithful and in control of my life story. He has the answers that I need. I'm trusting Him to reveal His will for my life in His perfect time.

So here's to everyone who's waiting on a dream of his or her heart to come true: Be encouraged. God loves you. He is Faithful to keep all of His promises that are found in His Word (The Holy Bible). If He made a promise to you then you can trust Him to keep it. It's like my Grandma says, "God may not come when you want Him to but He's *always* on time!"

Let's Pray: Dear God, Please help me to worship You while I wait. I know that Your timing is perfect. May Your will be done in my life. In Jesus' Name I pray, Amen.

The Gathering

A devotional written by Alexis A. Goring

"Let us hold fast the confession of our hope without wavering, for He who promised is faithful. And let us consider one another in order to stir up love and good works, not forsaking the assembling of ourselves together, as is the manner of some, but exhorting one another, and so much the more as you see the Day approaching."
— Hebrews 10:23-25 (NKJV)

Shopping a few days after Christmas with my Mom at our favorite mall, I noticed a big crowd congregating inside a store, poring over the latest technology. I looked up and saw that the store was nameless. There was no visible sign to describe what it was, so I turned to my Mom and asked, "Is that an Apple Store?" My Mom immediately said, "Of course. What other store brings people together like that?"

A light bulb turned on and I made an instant connection between that reality and our reality as mere mortals living in a fallen world. It is very common for people to crowd into an Apple Store and pore over all the latest technology. However, it is very *uncommon* for people to flock to church, fill the pews from the front to the back of the sanctuary, and press into Jesus Christ, allowing His restoring love to pour into our broken hearts.

Why is it that we're so quick to get the latest technology and stay up to date with it at an Apple Store, but so reluctant to read a Bible and stay in touch with the Author (God)?

I know that we all may be guilty of not spending enough time with God. But think about it. We make time for what matters to us and God should matter most.

People gather religiously at sporting events, favorite stores, cafes, restaurants, and movie theaters. Why don't people flock to church to gather together before the Lord?

Jesus brings people together. His Gathering is of greater purpose than The Apple Store. Why pore over new technology like your life depends on it when you can pore over God's Word and be transformed from the inside out? Most importantly, our life *does* depend on it.

When Jesus Christ ministered here on Earth, large crowds gathered to hear Him preach about the now and the not yet. He told stories that taught kingdom principles—God's Kingdom principles.

Jesus served food that never faded. He served heavenly manna (Matthew 4:4), words of wisdom to help get you through this life on Earth. His words can help you get into heaven.

Best of all, Jesus is not just a Bible character. He is real. Those characters whose stories are told in the Bible are dead now but the Lord still lives! And He is constantly wooing our hearts to His. He wants us to gather around Him, learn from His life lessons, then go tell the world about Him and His saving grace.

"Jesus is Coming Again" is more than a church hymn. It's a promise. And He keeps His promises!

So won't you gather before the Lord in His church? All He asks is for you to meet Him there once a week. But He does not want church to be your only interaction with Him. He wants you to daily spend time in His presence, read His Word (The Holy Bible) that's better than all the latest technology, and follow His instructions.

Most of all, He wants you to tell the world about Him because His Gathering is all-inclusive. He wants *everyone* to be saved.

I found that going to God's Gathering refreshes my soul and renews my spirit. I can get from God want I cannot get from the Apple Store. I can get peace that passes all understanding (Philippians 4:7), complete joy (John 15:11), and guidance from this life to the next (Proverbs 3:5-6).

Won't you go to God's Gathering? He's waiting to welcome you with open arms!

Let's Pray: *Dear God, Thank You for promising to be in the midst of Your people when we gather together to worship You (Matthew 18:20). Please help us to always seek You in Bible study, prayer and through gathering with our fellow believers in Bible-based churches led by pastors who You've called to lead, guide, and encourage us through this life here on Earth. In Jesus' Name I pray, Amen.*

God Knows Your Name

"For I know the plans I have for you," declares the Lord, "plans to prosper you and not to harm you, plans to give you hope and a future."
– Jeremiah 29:11 (NIV)

Pastor Charles A. Tapp shared a story one Sabbath morning, as a sermon illustration for his congregation.

He talked about how when he was about to graduate from school with his M.Div. (Master of Divinity) which is a degree that he needed to be a pastor, his fellow theology students were gathered around talking about how they know this person and that person who will give them a job when they graduate. Pastor Tapp said they turned to him and asked, "Charles, who do you know?" Without skipping a beat, Pastor Tapp said, "I know God."

Years later, this sermon illustration returned to my mind in relation to my search for a job in my career field. I earned a B.A. in Print Journalism and an MFA in Creative Writing. I've trained all of the talents the God gave me through studying for these degrees. But the dream job has not yet materialized.

So for a while, I've been trying to do what a lot of aspiring creative professionals do—reach out the big names in the business, the famous ones who have a proven track record of success because as someone told me last year, "Once Oprah knows your name, you're good." They mean that if Oprah knows your name and likes your work, she can open doors and do wonders for your career.

But lately, I am reminded of that sermon illustration and my Mom's advice. My Mom told me, "Why are you trying to network with all of the big names in the industry? Just network with God because He knows everybody."

A song by one of my favorite Contemporary Christian music singers comes to mind. The song is called "He Knows My Name", and Francesca Battistelli sings it.

The essence of the song is that we are less than perfect. We might not choose ourselves to be on a winning team or celebrated as a champion so we think that God should choose somebody else. But God sees our heart. He made us which means He knows exactly what we need and when we need it.

The song points out that you don't need your "name in lights" (which means to be well-known due to your work in the Arts & Entertainment industry) because you're already famous in God's eyes and He knows your name.

It's comforting because it reminds me of what really matters and teaches me that even if my name is never in lights, I will be more than okay because

God knows my name. He will take care of me whether it's blessing me with my dream job or opening my eyes to something He has planned that is better than what I've imagined.

Ultimately, I realize that God knows my name and He is in control of my destiny. I choose to trust Him to lead me to the job that He knows I need.

Are you experiencing something similar? Let me encourage you to reach out to God. He loves you with all of His heart and He can connect you with the right people to make your dreams come true. He will place you in the best situations and bless you with what you need. It may be something that you never even knew you wanted.

Let's Pray: Dear God, Thank You that You know my name. Please bless me with exactly what I need, exactly when I need it. I choose to trust You as my Divine Connection. Thank You for blessing me with my life. May I use my life to honor You, obey You and bring glory to You. Please bless me with the career that You made me for and help me to always keep in mind that I work for You, Lord. In Jesus' Name I pray, Amen.

Alexis A. Goring is a passionate writer with a degree in Print Journalism and an MFA in Creative Writing. She loves the art of storytelling and hopes that her stories will connect readers with the enduring, forever love of Jesus Christ.

Facebook: https://www.facebook.com/AuthorAlexisAGoring/
Twitter: https://twitter.com/PennedbyAlex
Website: https://alexisagoring.jimdo.com
Pinterest: https://www.pinterest.com/capturingidea/
Goodreads: https://www.goodreads.com/author/show/7260528.Alexis_A_Goring
"God is Love"
blog: http://capturingtheidea.blogspot.com

I Feed Angels

By: Sheila S. Hudson

I feed angels on a regular basis. At least that's what I choose to believe.

The first time it happened I had just exited the doctor's office when I heard a voice, a low muffled voice that startled me.

"I won't hurt you, Lady."

The face accompanying the voice seemed kind. For some reason I believed him. My heart beat wildly in my chest as he explained that he and his \friend were hungry. It was lunchtime and I could relate. He said they hadn't had anything to eat in two days. I couldn't relate to that! The strangers vowed that they wanted jobs, but no one would hire them.

The word "hungry" hovered thick in the air. Like eager puppies, they waited for my response. Their eyes were so vacant and hollow that I wanted to believe them. I knew what Jesus would do, but was I brave enough to follow through?

Quickly my mind and brain functioned in tandem.

"I can't give you any money, but I'll buy you lunch," I said. Why I said that, I don't know. It seemed right. When I suggested that they meet me at a fast food place across the street, they nodded in agreement.

As I got into my car, I wondered if I'd been "taken." Would they show up or disappear because I didn't offer cash. As I pulled into the parking lot, they were patiently waiting. Like obedient children, the men waited as I entered the store, purchased the lunches and brought them out. They accepted them, thanking me all the while. I talked to them for a bit, trying to direct them to community resources where they might bathe and change clothes maybe even get a job of some kind. When we parted, I felt in my soul that I had obeyed Jesus' mandate.

Onlookers smiled and nodded. A restaurant worker tipped his hat to me. One human being helping another. Why is it so unusual that the world takes time to notice? I held my head a little higher for the rest of the day.

Today it happened again. On many of my trips to Publix I have seen a person with a sign "will work for food." Every time I pass him I want to do something to help, today I did. Risking a lane change and a honk from other drivers, I pulled to the curb, lowered my windshield, and offered him a twenty. He sprinted to the side of my car and with tearful eyes accepted my money with a "God bless you."

I realize that my "feeding angels" campaign is like a band aid on an arterial flow, but my soul compels me to do something. Jesus said, "If we do it to the least of these, we have done it unto Him." Scriptures remind us that many "entertain angels unaware."

Perhaps I flunked the test. Maybe I am the most gullible person in town. But nothing in me could turn away from desperate, hollow eyes.

I probably will never know what happened to any of those I've given food or money to. Perhaps they are professional hucksters who get "free lunch" every day. Or maybe just maybe they are truly down on their luck. Perhaps I win the Ms. Gullible award, but I prefer to think that I feed angels.

Putting the Punch in Your Prayer Life

By: Sheila S. Hudson

> *. . . During a visit to England, I found myself wandering the stacks of a theological library. Impulsively, I picked a 19th-century autobiography from a shelf. The book described the life of an obscure vicar. But what grabbed me was a newspaper clipping . . . the vicar's obituary.*
>
> *I read, 'The vicar was a man of prayer. He loved to pray for his congregation.* **People came from all around to hear him pray for them. And as they listened, they were comforted and learned to pray by his example.'** *I was jolted.* **'People came from all around to hear him (not preach!) pray.'** *Who, I asked myself, would ever come to our church to hear me pray?*

Gordon MacDonald, Spring 2012, Leadership Journal.

If we took a poll, I believe it would show that prayer is the Christian's most underused weapon in our spiritual arsenal. Prayer is commonly reserved for disasters, crises of gigantic proportions, and lives spiraling out of control. The American philosophy of self –reliance has so penetrated the church that we view prayer as the last resort.

Many of us were raised on the adage, *Prayer Changes Things,* but Oswald Chambers begs to differ: *To say that 'prayer changes things' is not as close to the truth as saying, 'Prayer changes me and then I change things.'"*

The scripture is filled with prayers that change people who change things. Esther fortified her life with prayer support and risked her life to save her people. Prayer fortified Daniel in the lion's den and Shadrach, Meshach, and Abednego in the fiery furnace. Hezekiah's faithful prayers gained him 15 years of life. Prayer changed the prophets, the disciples, and the early Christians but does it change me? Beside those warriors of faith, my prayer life is anemic. I admit that I am a praying failure but I suspect that I am not alone.

Today is a world filled with clutter, confusion, and complication. Even well-intentioned Christians never quite get around to praying like we desire. We routinely perform tasks with half-empty spiritual tanks. Having a regular devotional time is a challenge. Consistent failure to carve out time leads to discouragement all the while our prayer life grows weaker or perhaps nonexistent. Our communion with the One who loves us warts and all is non-negotiable if we desire power, urgency, nonstop communication, courage, and honesty in our prayer life.

When it comes to powerful praying, few could match Elijah. The book of James tells us of Elijah's petitions to stop the rain. He got the attention of God's people through a drought.

POWER: *Elijah was a man just like you. He prayed earnestly that it would not rain and it did not rain on the land for three and a half years. Again he prayed and the heavens gave rain and the earth produced its crops[i].*

Elijah was filled with the Holy Spirit. God's people were in the midst of desperate times and Elijah executed desperate measures, measures which could jeopardize his life. God did as Elijah asked and no moisture came for three and a half years. He honored Elijah's request.

Jesus commanded us to pray with power. *Jesus replied, I tell you the truth, if you have faith and do not doubt, not only can you do what was done to the fig tree, but also you can say to this mountain, 'Go, throw yourself into the sea,' and it will be done. If you believe, you will receive whatever you ask for in prayer[ii]*

URGENCY: In I Kings 17-19[iii] Elijah made sure that God's people understood what was happening. He didn't chalk it up to chance or fate or environmental changes. He made sure they knew that God withhold the dew and the rain because of His wrath toward their pagan worship.

Elijah's stand didn't make him popular but he was respected especially after the showdown with the prophets of Baal at Mount Carmel. Only after the victory at Mount Carmel did Elijah pray for rain. And his prayers were answered.

We have many urgent things in our life. Sometimes the tyranny of the urgent overrules the important. Let us never forget Jesus' words in John 14-17 as Jesus reminds us, *I do not pray for these alone but also for those who will believe in Me through their word; that they may all be one, as You, Father, are in Me, and I in You; that they also may be one is Us, that the world may believe that You sent Me.[iv]* Whenever I remember that Jesus prayed for ME I am encouraged to do the same for others.

NON-STOP: Fortunately, James doesn't end his remarks about prayer with this account. In James 4:16 he challenges his audience to pray when they are in trouble, sick, happy, or in need of confession. Then he ends with the promise: *The prayer of a righteous man is* *powerful and effective.*[v]

No study of prayer would be complete without Paul's admonition to ". . . *Rejoice always, pray continually, give thanks in all circumstances; for this is God's will for you in Christ Jesus.*[vi]

CONFESSION: God's scheme of redemption is the theme throughout the Bible. God's grace and forgiveness overflows to mankind yet sometimes man is blind to our need.

If we confess our sins, he is faithful and just and will forgive us our sins and purify us from all unrighteousness.[vii]

The only one who hates restoration, peace, and forgiveness is the Deceiver. God chose Elijah, Daniel, Esther, Moses and others like them to deliver his people and ready them for the Messiah. We have the advantage of a model in Jesus. He exemplified what the Hebrew writer penned: *Let us then approach God's throne of grace with confidence, so that we may receive mercy and find grace to help us in our time of need.*[viii]

HONESTY: *My brothers if one of you should wander from the truth and someone should bring him back, remember this: Whosoever turns a sinner from the error of his way will save him from death and cover over a multitude of sins.*[ix]

Honest relationships in prayer are the only ones who bear fruit. James warns that if you ask for something you must believe. If we doubt *that man should not think he will receive anything from the Lord; he is a doubled minded man, unstable in all he does.*[x]

We are encouraged to ask and to seek and to knock. Prayer is as essential as oxygen t to the Christian. Doubt has no place in my prayers. I must petition with power, urgency, confession, and honesty. I must learn to 'pray without ceasing.'

In *Letters to Malcolm: Chiefly on Prayer,* C. S.

Lewis confides: *Relying on God has to begin all over again every day as if nothing had yet been done.*[xi]

And therein is our hope. Reliance on Him must be daily, without question, continual, and renewable. I want prayers with PUNCH. How about you?

Sheila S. Hudson is the author of the Thursday Club series: *Murder at Golden Palms, Murder at Sea, Murder at the Mandelay, Murder at the Monastery, Murder on the Marquee,* and *Murder under the Christmas Tree* published by Take Me Away Books.

Sheila is also the author of *Classic City Murders: Volumes I and II* published by ThomasMax Publishers, Inc. Her first publications were two nonfiction books: *13 Decisions That Will Change Your Life* and *13 Decisions That Will Transform Your Marriage* (Dancing with Bear Publishing). Sheila has contributed to *Not Your Mother's Book* (2*), Chocolate for Women* (8), *Chicken Soup, Patchwork Path* (2*), Love Stories* (2) plus numerous periodicals.

All are available at www.amazon.com or on her website www.sheilahudsonwriter.com

Her byline also appears in Purple Pros and Costumer Magazine. Bright Ideas, the parent company, was established to bring hope and inspiration through the written/spoken word. Since 1983, Sheila has been affiliated with Southeastern Writers Association including two terms as president. Contact her at: sheilahudson.writer@gmail.com; Sheila@13decisions.com or visit www.13decisions.com or www.sheilahudsonwriter.com for information on speaking engagements and forthcoming books.

Sheila and her husband, Timothy L. Hudson, have worked in campus ministry for over 30 years -- 5 years with Christian Student Fellowship at Northern Kentucky University and 28 years at Christian Campus Ministry at the University of Georgia. They have been married for 49 years and have two daughters, a son, and seven grandsons.

Good Morning Lord!

By Janetta Fudge-Messmer

"You awaken me morning by morning, wakens my ear to listen like one being taught. My Sovereign Lord has opened my ears, and I haven't been rebellious; I have not drawn back." (Isa. 50:4-5).

Not another morning, Lord. NO!!! You can't make me get up. I don't want to face another day. I say these words and I'm sure they're familiar to you.

Reread my paraphrase – *You awaken me morning by morning.* What a wonderful image of the Lord standing there at the foot of your bed, gently waking you up. Much better than an old alarm clock blaring in our ears.

He wakes my ears to listen like one being taught. Soft words emanating, soothing my soul, hearing His still small voice, wanting to know more.

Morning by morning, I'm awaken by Him.
To listen and learn from my King.
Morning by morning, He awakens me.
Wakens my ear to listen and learn from Him.
Keeping me from evil and a rebellious heart.
Drawing back to Him and away from sin.

Words of My Mouth

By Janetta Fudge-Messmer

"May the words of my mouth and the meditation of my heart be pleasing in your sight, O Lord, my Rock and my Redeemer." (Psalm 19:14 NIV)

Friday afternoon I waited for the carpet installers to arrive. When they did, I pointed out the three rooms it would be installed in. One tricky area needed extra explanation, but with our language differences I'm not sure the man understood.

As I closed my front door an unsettling thought popped into my head. Did he *really* grasp my special instructions? I turned and reached for the door knob, muttering under my breath, "I wish companies would send people who speak English."

The second I said the harsh words, the verse in my morning devotional rushed back to me. "May the words of my mouth and the meditation of my heart be pleasing in your sight, O Lord, my Rock and my Redeemer."

I let go of the knob and asked the Lord for forgiveness and to help me trust Him for my carpet installation. A few hours later I returned, and all my worries evaporated. The gentleman and his crew understood. They crossed our language barrier with a job done to perfection.

Lord, forgive me and my judgment call. Instead of getting frustrated at the man, I needed to remember he had as much trouble understanding me. Amen.

Answered Prayers

By Janetta Fudge-Messmer

"Be joyful always; pray continually; give thanks in all circumstances, for this is God's will for you in Christ Jesus." (1 Thessalonians 5:16-18 NIV)

My right shoulder started giving me problems six months ago. When I winced at the slightest movement, my husband asked, "When are you going to the doctor to check this out?" My response, "If I ignore it, maybe it will go away."

It didn't go anywhere. And it told me so very LOUDLY one afternoon while helping Ray load up my little pick-up. I threw a piece of drywall with my "bad" arm and the searing pain almost brought me to my knees. I stood sobbing in my garage. Again, my husband asked me about going to the doctor. I assured him I'd make the appointment when I got home.

The reasons I put off calling the doctor was because I was scared. I didn't want to find out I needed surgery, but I couldn't deal with the intense pain any longer. I called and the appointment was set for a week later.

While I waited, I prayed fervently for healing for my shoulder. Also Ray and I went to Wednesday night service and I asked for prayer. Each night before I'd go to sleep I'd pray for healing. Me and the Lord spent quality time together discussing the possible outcome of

40

my shoulder problem.

It's just like the Lord; He decided to crank it up a notch. He suggested I pray for others when my shoulder bothered me. I did and in days I noticed my pain diminished to an occasion pang, but I kept praying (with a very thankful heart) for myself, family and friends.

I ended up having an MRI done. The day I'd find out the results, Ray and I had to wait an hour before they called us back to the examining room. I prayed without ceasing.

The doctor came in and said, "You don't need surgery. Physical therapy will do the trick." I almost jumped off the table and kissed him. My tears this time were tears of joy. My prayers were answered.

Prayer works, and I continue to thank the Lord for bringing me through my pain with joy, prayer and thanksgiving.

Prayer: Thank You, Lord, for answered prayers. Thank You that I can come to You for whatever is going on and You will hear me. I ask for healing for my friends and family. Please bless them as only You can do. Amen!

Subtle Fragrances

By Janetta Fudge-Messmer

"But the fruit of the Spirit is love, joy, peace, patience, kindness, goodness, faithfulness, gentleness and self-control." (Galatians 5:22a NIV)

I caught a whiff of the subtle fragrance of Jergen's lotion. The familiar aroma reminded me of my mother and how she smelled after smoothing the creamy lotion on her delicate hands.

For a moment I savored the sweet, wonderful memories of her and her arms encircled me in a hug. All is well in my world once again.

Another scent believers should recognize is the fragrance of the Holy Spirit. Its perfume beckons us to allow it to permeate our soul with the fruit of the Spirit of God.

Love, joy, peace, patience, kindness, goodness, faithfulness, gentleness and self-control. His fruit touches us with the message of hope, and transformation all the days of our lives.

Thank you, Lord, for the gift of your Holy Spirit. Let its fragrance surround me as I share your bountiful harvest with others. Amen!

Dimness into Light

By Janetta Fudge-Messmer

"Then Jesus spoke again to the people, he said, "I am the light of the world. Whoever follows me will never walk in the darkness, but will have the light of life." (John 8:12 NIV)

Last week my computer screen went dim. For no apparent reason. My immediate thought – I'd somehow turned down the dimmer. I pushed on the plus sign with the cute little light bulb on it. My screen stayed in its dimmed state.

What could I do, but seek a higher power? My hubby. The computer guru I've learned to trust with all the issues I run into.

After a few clicks of the mouse and a question or two to our techie friend, Ray solved my problem. Now the brightness on my screen almost blinded me. I had to turn it down a smidge to even work on it.

I thanked my sweetie for his superb work, but as I typed on my new-and-improved screen I thought, "How many times are we 'dim' (out of sorts with life)?"

Do we wallow in the biggest pity party or do we seek a Higher Power…(God)…to help us when we're skidding out of control? Or when we're close to hitting rock bottom? Do we stand and wonder what our next move should be in all the mess?

It's GOD in our dimness.

It's GOD in our weakness.

It's GOD in in our darkness.

He sees past our hurts to bring healing to our souls.

Today, let's seek Him. Yes, the Lord will take us out of darkness into His glorious light.

AMEN!!!

Early Birds, Southbound Birds, Girly Birds and Blessing Bird) are sure to make you laugh out loud. They may also make you want to hit the road in your own RV. Janetta, her hubby (Ray), and their pooch (Maggie) are full-time RVers. Writing and traveling go hand in hand as they see the USA in their twenty-five foot Minnie Winnie.

LINKS:

Available on Amazon: https://goo.gl/rd0X4T
E-mail: janettafudgemessmer@gmail.com
Website: http://janettafudgemessmer.com/
Blog: http://www.nettie-fudges-world.blogspot.com/
Facebook:
https://www.facebook.com/janetta.fudge.messmer
Twitter: https://twitter.com/nettiefudge

I'm Here!

By Linda Baten Johnson

Read Deuteronomy 31:6-8
And surely I am with you always, to the very end of the age. Matthew 28:20 (NIV)

My granddaughter Krista loves to hide and then pop out from unexpected places--a darkened pantry, from behind a bathroom shower curtain, or from underneath a pile of clothes in the closet. When I get close to her hiding spot, she jumps out and joyfully declares "I'm here!" After my heart stops racing from her surprise appearance, I give her a hug, happy to see her, and grateful that she is with me.

We often seek God's presence in the difficult moments of our lives, when the darkness is overpowering, when we are in unexpected situations, or overwhelmed by the clutter and mess of our current situation. Unlike Krista, God does not hide. He is always here, ready to embrace and love us.

Thought for the Day

God is always with us.

Prayer: Father, we thank you for the constant love and care you offer us. We ask that you show us a specific person that we might encourage with loving care today. Amen.

> *Prayer Focus:* **Grandchildren learning about God.**

Encouragers

By Linda Baten Johnson

Read Exodus 17: 8-13

In Paul's letters, he often names the friends who helped him and he expresses his love and appreciation for these encouragers. In the Old Testament scripture featured today, Moses needed physical support and encouragement from Aaron and Hur. During the battle, when Moses became so weary that he could no longer hold his hands up, they steadied his arms so that Joshua's army could win the battle.

Those who helped Paul allowed him to do the work God called him to do. We all need encouragement, and we all need to be encouragers.

THOUGHT FOR THE DAY

Offer words of encouragement to someone today.

Prayer: **Father, we thank you for the encouragement we have received from others, and we ask that you show us a specific person for us to support or encourage today. Amen.**

Prayer Focus: **Those who need encouragement.**

God Be You

By Linda Baten Johnson

Read 1 John 4:7-21

You show that you are a letter from Christ, the result of our ministry, written not with ink, but with the Spirit of the living God, not on tablets of stone but on tablets of human hearts.
2 Corinthians 3:3 (NIV)

I attended the early service rather than my regular one. I arrived late and slipped into a seat near the back of the sanctuary just before the call to worship. The young man sitting in the same row of chairs seemed to be in fervent prayer. During announcements, he thumbed through his well-worn Bible stopping to read certain passages. He sang the hymns joyously, and gave the responses firmly, with much emotion. My own worship was heightened because I shared the experience with a young man I'd never met.

Toward the close of the service, I passed him a note asking if he had a special need for prayers in the coming week. He wrote back asking me to pray that his family would find a home, and he signed his name beneath the words "God Be You."

The words startled me. Did he mean to write God Bless You instead of God Be You? I don't know. But his answer reminded me of the hymn *Let Others See Jesus in You*. I saw God in the young man's attentive attitude that morning. I could have said to him "God be you." The words, which might have been a careless mistake, made me ask myself the question from the chorus of that hymn: Do others see Jesus in me?

THOUGHT FOR THE DAY

Your life's a book before their eyes,
They're reading it through and through. Say does it point them to the skies? Do others see Jesus in you?

From: *Let Others See Jesus in You*

Prayer: Father, help us to live so that people will know we are Christians by our love and our lives. Amen.

Prayer Focus: Those who need prayers and help.

Cheerful Giving

Deuteronomy 15:7-11

Mother's tithing bowl was a glass pie plate in the cabinet above the toaster. Ten percent on any income from babysitting, making pies, ironing, or working as a cook in the local café went straight into the bowl. When I was in elementary school, I begged my mother to use the tithing money to purchase me a dress for a special occasion.

Mother explained that she couldn't use the tithing money because that was her way of thanking God for the riches our family enjoyed--healthy bodies, capable minds, a productive garden, a supportive church community, good friends, but most of all God's own great love. Paul says in 2 Corinthians 9:7 that God loves a cheerful giver. My mother lived her belief of giving cheerfully, and her example enriched the faith of her family and friends.

Thought for the Day

Count your blessings

Instead of your woes.

Prayer: **Dear God and Father, thank you for the rich blessings we have been given and guide us as we respond to Your love with our gifts and our service. Amen.**

Prayer Focus: **Cheerful givers**

Linda Baten Johnson grew up in White Deer Texas, where she won blue ribbons for storytelling. She still loves telling tales. A tornado destroyed the town when Linda lived there, and watching faith-based actions in rebuilding lives and homes after tragedy influences her writing.

She writes for young readers who face difficult situations and for the romantic reader who prefers the squeaky-clean version of love.

Visit her website at www.lindabatenjohnson.com or the Amazon author profile or the Facebook author page.
Email Linda at lindabatenjohnson123@gmail.com.

My Right Hand God!

By Patty Smith Hall

But when Jesus overheard what was said, he told the synagogue leader, "don't be afraid. Only believe."
Mark 5:36

"Y ou're afraid."
This wasn't the first time someone had said this to me, and I'm certain it won't be the last. For while I am confident in most areas of my life, I'm a stinking coward when it comes to those things that matter only to me.

Like my singing.

Growing up, I loved to sing, especially outside on our front porch swing. I would sing for hours, memorizing the songs from all the old musicals like Oklahoma and South Pacific. So it was natural for me to join the chorus when I entered middle school. Finally, I could sing my heart out! But a few weeks in, my best friend pulled me aside and told me the truth.

I didn't sing very well.

I was heartbroken. Even as I grew older and was picked to sing solos at school and at church, her words reminded me of my inabilities. I suffered stage fright to the point I finally stopped singing. And those feelings didn't stop there. I began to question all my abilities. Had I only been selected for the ballet company because my teachers felt sorry for me? Is the writing I love to do really any good at all?

Which seems silly, doesn't it? I have a husband who I adore, two daughters and a son-in-law who I love more than words, and a grandson who gives me more joy than one heart can hold. My life is a shower of blessings despite the hurt and the pain that sometimes walks alongside me in this journey. So why am I so afraid when it comes to something like writing a simple story?

Because with my words, my heart is laid out for all to see, naked and vulnerable. What if readers don't like what I have to say? Worse still, what if I disappoint God?

In my studies of verses pertaining to fear, this one in Isaiah 41 spoke to me-"For I, Yahweh your God, hold your right hand and say to you, do not be afraid, I will help you." According to this scripture, God is holding my hand and not just any hand, but my right hand. The one that holds my pen when I write. He knows every phrase, every word that I put to paper. He's wrapped around me, holding my unsteady hand. He takes my fear and encourages me, pushing me toward the goal. Any successes I have is all due to Him.

Because He is my right-hand man!

More reading--Mark 5:35-42

Prayer--Lord, our world is full of situations that cause fear to hang over us like a heavy burden. Help us to recognize your presence surrounding us, to fill your hand on hours and to follow your command--do not be afraid!

Finding Hope in the Pit of Despair

By Patty Smith Hall

Why am I so depressed? Why this turmoil within me?
Put your hope in God, for I will still praise him, my
Savior and my God.

Psalms 42:5

A lot of people don't know this, but I've lived through bouts of depression for the majority of my life. It's not something I like to talk about or that I take lightly. Growing up, I witnessed both my mother and my grandmother suffered nervous breakdowns that required hospitalization. As a young girl, I made a battle plan to fight. I looked at my bouts of depression as a lifelong war, a battle I wager every second of each day.

Depression isn't just worrying about something, though that's part of it. It's about feeling hopeless in your worries, obsessing about the worst-case scenarios, playing them out in your mind. It's a very lonely place to be because you feel that no one could possibly understand what you're going through.

One of the weapons I use to get me to those rough moments is reading Psalms written by King David. Here was a deeply faithful man favored by God who struggled with "anxious concerns" and "agony in my mind every day." (Psalms 13:2-3) He was "bent over and brought low all day long, mourning (Psalms 38:6.) He was "faint and severely crushed, I groan because of the anguish of my heart" (Psalms 38:8.) He was weary from his groaning, with his tears he dampened his pillow and drenched his bed every night (Psalms 6:6.)

Yet, this what David does in response to his depression that gives those of us who suffer away out at the mired pit of destruction--he turned to the Lord for help. Psalms 6:8-9 says the Lord hears the sound of our weeping and our plea for help. He accepts our prayers. Psalms 13; five – eight states that David "trusted in your fateful love and his heart rejoiced in your deliverance." David asked God in Psalms 38; 22 two hurried to help him.

Being depressed doesn't mean that you're any less faithful to God or dealing with unrepentant sin. But it is an opportunity to grow closer to the Lord when you are at your most vulnerable. God is there with you in your struggle, holding you up, putting your feet on solid ground. Don't be afraid to call upon him for help, even if it means crying out every moment of every day. God is there for you, holding you up, loving you with all his heart.

Additional reading—Psalms 38

Prayer--Lord, my struggles with depression doesn't come as a surprise to you. Help me focus on you; clear my mind of wayward thoughts. I praise you for what you were doing in my life

It Only Gets Better.

By Patty Hall Smith

And they become one flesh.
Genesis 2:24

I don't know a woman who doesn't love a wedding. The look on the groom's face as he sees his bride for the first time. The vows promised. While all that is wonderfully romantic, I love to hear the wedding toast from the bride or groom. It's always very sweet--about how the groom noticed his new wife from across a crowded room or how she felt like she was the luckiest woman in the world. It usually ends with them saying, "This is the happiest day of my life."

Sorry to burst your bubble, but it's not. Not by a long shot!

One might ask me how I could possibly say such a thing. Well, my husband, Danny and I just celebrated our 35th wedding anniversary, and we're happier today than we were on our long-ago wedding day. Not every day of the past 35 years have been a walk in the park--life-threatening pregnancy complications, a disabling back injury, and the pain and embarrassment of the foreclosure. We endured separations, both work related and those of our making, and we still have bills to pay.

But there have been great times too: the excitement of buying our first home together, the wonder of watching our girls be born, relishing our roles as empty-nesters, and the joy of our first grandchild. There's also the simple everyday things that reminds me of how much Danny loves me. Like when he used his allowance to buy wallpaper when I wanted to decorate but we couldn't afford it or when he walks in the door looking for me because as he says that's the best part of his day. He respects me, confides in me and dreams big dreams for me. I just pray I'm is good to him.

God knew what he was doing when he came up with marriage. He has handpicked someone just for you-- "houses and welts are inherited from parents, but a prudent wife is from the Lord." The marriage relationship is often compared to our own relationship with Christ--Ephesians 5:22-23. When we marry, we are no longer two, but one flesh (Matthew 19:4-6 we become bone of his bone and flesh of his flesh.) As wives, we are to submit (not serve!) to them as we would to the Lord while our husbands should live with us in the understanding way, showing honor to us loving us as Christ loves his church (1 Peter 3:1-5, 7)

Yes, Danny and I are happier today than we were on our wedding day, and we'll be even more so in five years than we are today. Because we're living out those vows we made to each other, loving each other 'until death do us part."

Additional Reading--Ephesians 5:22-33

Prayer—Lord, thank you for this man I've married. Help me to nurture our relationship, giving my whole self to him so that we can truly be as one flesh. Make me the wife described in Proverbs 31:10-31, Lord.

Burnout!

By Patty Smith Hall

Therefore, my heart was glad, and my tongue rejoiced.
Moreover, my flesh will rest in hope.
Acts 2:26

R est.
The word jumped off the page of my Sunday school lesson. The last few months, I'd wavered between burnout and depression, my body spirit and mine so weary, it felt like a chore to even breathe at times. Confused by my lack of energy, I struggled. Why had the two things that give me so much joy--my desire to write and to go to church--suddenly vanished into thin air?

I began to wonder what Jesus meant when He said, "Come all who are weary and rest." Being the researcher that I am, I looked deeper into the verse and was surprised by what I learned.

Rest and restoration are common thread throughout Scripture, highlighting the importance in God's eyes. It doesn't just involve the physical, the mind and the soul. It is so important to God that he showed us by example how to rest in Genesis 1--on the seventh day, God rested and saw that his work was very good. Rest allows us to renew our minds, body and spirit, restoring to us more strength and focus.

I understood that, but how does one rest one's soul?

In the amplified Bible, Matthew 11:28 is explained this way. "Come to me, all of you who labor and are heavy laden and overburdened, and I will cause you to rest; I will ease and refresh your soul." Heavy latent and overburdened--three words that describe most of us these days. Between the constant responsibilities at home and work, of caring for aging parents and raising fate filled children, of worries and inside these about the imperfect world we live in, how can we find rest for our beleaguered souls?

Only in Jesus. As it says in Matthew 11:30, "his yoke is light, wholesome, useful, good--not harsh, sharp or pressing, and his burden light. What that means for us is that we have to trust him with those things that make us so sick and worried. We have to lay them down to his feet, crawl into his lap and leaned on his strong shoulders.

Because we can't find rest on our own.

Only then, when we give our trust fully to him will we receive the blessed rest our soul craves.

Additional reading—Psalms 62:5-8

Prayer—Lord, you know the worry and stress that troubles our hearts and robs us of our rest, both physically and spiritually. Teach me to lean on you, to find restoration in the truth of Your never-ending love.

Everyone has an Opinion

By Patty Smith Hall

The fear of the Lord is the beginning of knowledge; fools despise wisdom and discipline.
Proverbs 1:7

Reading through the article on NFL players' decision to kneel during the playing of our national anthem made my blood boil. Not because they didn't have the right to bring attention to their social cause—according to US Constitution, everyone has the right to peacefully protest. Even the Bible speaks of prayerful protest as in the case of the Right to Life movement.

No, my beef with this particular article were the thoughtlessness responses shown to people who disagreed. The name calling and general ugliness sent my temper soaring to the point that I wrote my own biting response. But before I hit the send button, I realized something.

I was no better than the folks I wanted to condemn.

Proverbs is my favorite book in the Bible, mainly because I love its common sense and straight forward advice, and boy, does it address the problem of man's opinions. In Proverbs 18:2 that 'fools find no pleasure in understanding but delights in airing their own opinions.' Proverbs 1:22 says, 'How long, foolish ones, will you love ignorance? How long with you mockers enjoy mocking and you fools hate knowledge? How about Proverbs 12:23 which says, 'A shrewd person conceals knowledge, but a foolish heart publicizes stupidity.'

As living, breathing creations, God gave us the ability to seek knowledge, to think and to feel. But that doesn't give us the right to berate and insult someone else for having a different point-of-view than ourselves. So how do we do this? That's a three-part answer. First, by controlling our tongue-'When there are many words, sin is unavoidable, but the one who controls his lips is wise.'(Proverbs 10:19) We should be ready to listen to others voice their concerns-'My dearly loved brothers, understand this: Everyone must be quick to hear, slow to speak, and slow to anger.' (James 1:19) We must learn to control our temper-'Don't let your spirit rush to be angry, for anger abides in the heart of fools.'(Ecclesiastes 7:9)

I'm not going to lie—Controlling my tongue (or in my case, my keypad) is still hard at times. But if I want to be the woman God wants me to be, I need to remember how to answer any disagreement with the respect and love for others that God lays out in the Bible, or better yet, walk away rather than cause pain and damage my testimony.

Prayer—Lord, help me learn to control my tongue. Make my words respectful and loving, a testimony of Your grace inside of me.

Additional verses: Ecclesiastes 7

When Peace Seems Impossible

By Patty Smith Hall

*Come to Me, all of you who are weary and burdened,
and I will give you rest.*

Matthew 12:28

Sleep often alludes me. I'm not sure why I have this problem, only that it has plagued me since I was a young girl of eight. Then, I would walk around our house at all hours of the night, checking on my parents and my siblings, making sure all was well with them.

As I grew older, the problem grew worse. Nights would go by with me tossing and turning. I tried everything—listening to music, journaling my thoughts, wearing myself out until I thought I would drop. I even resorted to sleeping medication in hopes of just a couple of hours of sleep. But nothing worked.

I was at the end of my rope when my mother finally confronted me about my problem. Expecting her to take me to another doctor, I was surprised by her suggestion.

"Why don't you pray yourself to sleep?"

I'd never thought to pray about it. Why would God, who had so many other, more important things to do, help me fall asleep? Looking at another sleepless night, I climbed into bed with a sense of skepticism. But as I laid there, the vision of myself crawling into His lap, His arms curling around me and holding me close filled my senses. Leaning my head on His big chest, I began to pour out all my worries and concerns. My body relaxed, and before I finished, I was sound asleep.

Whether it's a sick family member, a stack of unpaid bills or the latest calamity being reported by the media, finding any kind of peace in this world is almost impossible. Our Heavenly Father wants us to find that elusive peace in Him. In 1 Peter 5:7, we're told to 'cast all your cares on Him, because He cares about you.' Colossians 3:15 says 'let the peace of the Messiah, to which you were also called in one body, control your hearts. Be thankful.' And my personal favorite, 'And the peace of God, which transcends all understanding, will guard your hearts and minds in Jesus Christ.'

It's hard to find peace in a world filled with such sin and strife, but God, in His uncompromising love, offers it to us if we just ask. So, climb up in our Father's lap, rest against Him and pour out your heart. He's listening, ready and willing to give you a peace that 'transcends all understanding.'

Prayer: Lord, sometimes, I let the noise of this world rob me of the peace You so freely give. Thank you for listening and offering the rest only You can give. Amen.

Additional Reading: Psalms 29:11

Pulling Spiritual Weeds

By Patty Smith Hall

*But the fruit of the Spirit is love, joy, peace, patience,
kindness, goodness, faith, gentleness, self-control.
Against such things there is no law.*

Galatians 5:22

Over the past year, I've taken up gardening. Now those who know me understand just how ridiculous this is. My black thumb is notorious for killing even the sturdiest week!

But I was determined. My family enjoys vegetables fresh for the garden, and now that my grandparents have passed on and my father gave up on his, it was time for me to pick up the hoe and spade.

Boy, is it hard work! My plot in the community garden was overrun with weed and small stones. Once I'd picked up all the rocks and pulled the weeds, it was time to build up the soil; to feed it all the nutrients my plants would need to grow and cover it with mulch to cut back on weed production.

As I pulled a particularly stubborn weed, I got to thinking how spiritual life is a lot like a garden. Sometimes, we get those pesky little sins which don't look like much on the surface but can choke the life out of our faith. Then we have those sins that are so deeply

67

rooted in our lives, we don't recognize the danger in them until we're in deep trouble. And the stones are like our hardened hearts that block our way to the Son, instead bringing evil which leads astray while eating bits and pieces out of our hearts.

But when we weed out those things that put a strangle-hold on our faith, when we feed on the Word of God, spend time with the Lord in prayer, we begin to grow and mature. We become strong enough to fight off the weeds of this world and lift our faces to the Father who gives us a harvest of love, joy, peace, patience, kindness, goodness, faithfulness, gentleness and self-control.

Prayer: Lord, open my eyes to the sinful weeds in my life that keep me from You, those that are easily seen and those that are so deeply rooted inside me that I can't see the wrongness of them. Soften my heart toward You and others. Help me implant myself in Your Word. In Jesus name, Amen.

Further reading—Galatians 5

Growing Asparagus

By Patty Smith Hall

For in this case the saying is true; 'One sows and another reaps.'
John 4:37

Both my daughter and I love asparagus. Sautéed with a touch of butter and salt, it's a wonderful treat for the body. So when I decided to grow a garden, it was the very first pack of seeds that I bought. After I fixed the beds, making sure my little plants would get just the right combination of sunshine and moisture, I planted my seedlings.

Then I waited.

And waited. And waited until finally my seedlings peaked their tiny heads through the mulch and blossomed into tall fern-like plants. Only there wasn't any asparagus. I waited some more. The summer flew by until it was October, and the first frost loomed in the forecast. With no harvest in sight, I cut back the tall plants.

It was only after talking to an experienced gardener that I learned a hard truth—asparagus will take up to three years to produce a vegetable.

We live in a world of instant gratification. We want what we want, and we want it NOW. As Christians, we expect nothing less. We sow the seeds of salvation in a world of unsaved family and friends, yet we expect an instant response, a declaration of giving their life to the Lord. When it doesn't happen like we'd hoped, we get frustrated and asked ourselves is we're doing something wrong.

That's where patience comes in. We have to trust that God's timing is perfect, that only He knows when a soul is ready to turn to Him. We might have to consider the fact that although we are laying the seeds, it may be we aren't meant to reap the harvest. What we must focus on is doing the job God has called us to do. Don't drown unbelievers in Christian platitudes, instead living out our faith in a way that they yearn to live as we do, with Christ in their heart.

We may never see the harvest we've sowed here on earth, but we will all rejoice together with our Lord in heaven when we're called home!

Further reading: John 4

Prayer: Lord, use me in the way You see fit, be that sowing seeds of salvation or walking a life of faith. Give me the patience needed to wait for Your timing. And thank You for the privilege of serving You.

The Pacifier Thief

By Patty Smith Hall

*So now I am no longer the one doing it, but it is sin
living in me.* Romans 7:17

It started with a call from our grandson's preschool.
There was a very serious situation they needed to
discuss with our oldest daughter. When could she get
there?

Worried that our boy could be ill or worse, Jennifer
throw all of her stuff in her car and hurried as fast as she
could(without breaking the law herself) to the school our
grandson had been going to for the past few months.
Parking the SUV, she grabbed her purse and ran inside.

And found our boy laughing and playing with the
other babies in the class! She turned to the lead teacher
who led her to a quiet corner of the classroom.

"We have a problem."

Over the last few days, the teachers had noticed that
several of the other baby's pacifiers had gone missing.
They didn't think much of it at first. Everyone who has
ever had a little one knows how easy it is to misplace
those things. But on this particular day, a little girl who
was extremely attached to her pacifier in the class. One
minute, she was happy as a lark, then suddenly she was
screaming. Her pacifier was nowhere in sight.

That's when one of the teachers noticed our boy crawling toward the bookcase, a pacifier in hand. After further investigation, they found no only her's but several others stuffed behind the bookcase!

My nine-month-old grandboy was a pacifier thief!

Carter's 'crime' reminded me how we are born with a sin nature. He's too young to know right from wrong—it's his parents' job to teach him that over the next few years. Yet, he chose to take something that wasn't his. It hadn't been taught to him. He came up with the idea all by himself but how? Since the time of Adam, we've all been born with the compulsion to sin. It's in our DNA.

Which means we need a Savior. No matter how good a person you try to be, you still live in sin. The only way to be reconciled with our Lord is through the sinless blood of Jesus Christ.

Further Reading: Romans 7:13-25

Prayer: Lord, I struggle daily with the sin nature I've been born with, 'practicing the evil that I do not want to do.' Fill my heart and life with You.

Jesus is my Favorite Women's Libber

By Patty Smith Hall

Christ has liberated us to be free. Stand firm then and don't submit again to the yoke of slavery
Galatians 5:1

I collect t-shirts. Whether it be from my college or an interesting place I visited while researching my books, I love shirts that capture my attention. My current favorite says 'Raised on Sweet Tea and Jesus!' So it's not unusual to see me wearing my favorite Jane Austin quote or an expression of my faith as I jet around town.

I also notice other people's shirts. In many ways, those graphic art designs or homey sayings tells you a great deal about a person and where their heart lies. It's one of the reasons I stopped a lady going into the Walmart at the beach last summer. Her t-shirt called out the Bible-thumping, women's libber that I am.

'Jesus is my favorite women's libber.'

What a profound statement! One that a number of women in this time of protest and marches might not agree with, but as women of faith, we need to look no further than Proverbs 31:10-31. The woman described there is a thoroughly modern woman, balancing her family and home(Verses 13-15) while also holding down a job(Verse 24.)She owes property(Verse 16) and uses the money to build her own business. Even with all her responsibilities, she doesn't forget her community, reaching out the poor and those in need(Verse 20.) The people talk well of her and her husband(Verse 23.) Her husband and her children never fear of going hungry or cold(Verses 14-15; 21.) They respect her and know how blessed they are to have her in their lives(Verses 28-29.)

But more importantly, this very busy, very modern woman is wise enough to know where her true freedom lies—with her Lord. 'Charm is deceptive, and beauty is fleeting, but a woman who fears the Lord will be praised.'

Christ died to give us eternal freedom from sin. He reconciled us to our Heavenly Father who gives us purpose in our lives. When I march, I want to march alongside my Jesus, the only One who truly liberates my soul.

Further Reading: Proverbs 31:10-31

Prayer: Lord, the Proverbs 31 woman seems like the unobtainable goal, but through You, with Your strength, I can do all things. Mold me into a woman after Your own heart. In Jesus name I pray, amen.

Patty Smith Hall is a multi-published author with Love Inspired Historical and Barbour Publishing. Married to her hero of 33+years, Danny, and the mother of two extraordinary women, she calls North Georgia her home.

http://patty-smith-hall.blogspot.com/

https://www.pattysmithhall.com/

https://www.amazon.com/Patty-Smith-Hall/e/B005KN8GG2

Laughter is Good for the Soul

By Birdie L. Etchison

The tendency to laugh at not only others but mostly myself began in fourth grade.

Lois Ann and I were the 'fatties' of the class. Everyone laughed when we tried to play Hopscotch on the playground during recess. While others huddled in their groups and pointed and jeered, Lois Ann and I became fast friends. Not that we made the mark of friendship with a sharp knife to let our blood intermingle –we were both too squeamish, to do that, which we discovered when I fell and scraped my knee – but friends we were.

One afternoon in class we looked up from our arithmetic books and our eyes locked. A tiny giggle started from deep within, followed by a giggle from Lois Ann. She clapped her hand over her mouth and tried to look back at her book. It was useless. I looked back at her, and she at me, and the giggling grew louder.

Miss Westling ordered us to stop.

We couldn't. And it didn't matter that everyone set their pencils down and stared. By now the sound had become more of a guffaw, and we both ended up sitting out in the hall with notes to take home.

We had fathers, but fathers then never tended to such small matters as notes sent home from school. At least not over the minor problem of giggling in class.

Miss Westling moved us apart. It didn't help. Shame couldn't make us stop. Trips to the principal's office didn't help, nor punishment at home.

I learned a lesson from that long ago day. Laughter soothes away a lot of hurts. We both hurt because we were shunned by classmates. We hurt because we were different. But different can be good. And we came to realize that we could survive in spite of everything, all because we could laugh.

Lois Ann moved away in junior high. I have no idea where. I wish I did, for it would be special to see if we still have that ability to make each other laugh.

As Mark Twain said:

The human race has one effective weapon – and that is laughter.

Just One of Those Mornings

For you are my rock and my fortress; therefore for Your name's sake, lead me and guide me. Psa.31-3.

By Birdie L. Etchison

Most of us think we can only experience joy when everything is going right.
It was one of those mornings when 'everything went wrong that could go wrong.' It usually starts the minute my feet hit the floor at 6am. Now I could sleep in until 7, but if I do that, I won't get much done, and I need to get things done.

Schedules. Goals. Lists. I made them all the night before with feet up, lying back in the recliner. It sounds so simple in that position. Of course I'll have time to clean the closet, answer those e-mails, write a chapter on my new book, and call mom. Coffee begins my day. The smell of it permeates the house and I can't wait to get that first cup. The second and third cups don't taste nearly as good, as the coffee sits in the pot and becomes Atlas-strong, dark enough to polish your shoes. I have one friend who never drinks more than two cups and dumps the rest of the pot. Another friend waits until her husband has half his face shaved before hollering out the bathroom door, "turn the coffee on now."

Now that's timing.

After pouring that first cup of coffee, I reach for the orange juice. If coffee is good, juice is the second best thing early in the morning. But not when the glass crashes to the floor. Ten minutes later, the floor is cleaner than it has been in months, and now my coffee is cold, so I pour a second cup which is never as good as the first. But I've already said that, haven't I? If I'd just left the peanut butter alone, things would have been fine. It's way high in fats and carbs. Slather it on a slice of bread and it's a no-no. Add jam an inch thick; double no-no. I hurry, because for some reason if I hurry, it seems better.

Just as I start to take a bite, the bread slips from my hand and lands gooey side to the floor, of course. That is my second clue that I should go back to bed and stay there for an indefinite amount of time. But I don't. I lose my car keys, spill more orange juice don't even ask me how, and then sit down and laugh. That's when laughter comes in handy. You can't cry, so all you can do is laugh. And so I know I am fortified and ready for what the rest of the day brings. More spills, more lost items, but a heart full of laughter because, hey, it's *my* kind of day. And it's only 6:45

"*Rejoice   in   all   things*

My prayer: "Guide me, help me, and show me, always. Amen"

Rusha, Rusha, Rusha...

By Birdie L. Etchison

"I will praise You, O Lord, among the peoples; I will sing to you unto the nations. I will sing to You among the nations." Psa. 57:9

*Nothing can be more useful to you than a determination not to be -He*nry David Thoreau

We rush here and rush there. Use the cell phone while in a store or walking down the street. Order a latte to go –Unload the dishwasher while helping a. child with homework. Pick up the kids from practice (dance, ball, play – doesn't matter what); eat on the run because there's more activity in the early evening.

Families pick up hamburgers from a drive-up. A kid I know finally talked his family into going inside, where they sat on plastic chairs and ate off of plastic trays on a plastic table. Maybe the drive-up was a better idea. Activities abound all day long. Heaven help us if we want an hour to relax. Relax? What is that? Does anyone even know? It's the hectic pace that causes stress and other health problems. But do we learn? We keep on our merry pace. A busy person is a happy person, yes?

When was the last time you really relaxed; took your brain off of overload and looked at the stars? Watched a sunset. Observed a spider weaving a web?

No time, people comment. *"There's no time for such silliness."*

Maybe there should be. If you can't get it all done in one day, add it to the next day's list. My friend Gail says she's still working on her April list and here it is July. That's okay. She'd made two excursions to the beach, took her grandson garage saleing, and has written three poems. That's progress. It's also contentment, a sense of accomplishment. We need more of it.

I refuse to rush, to dash to hurry to anything. If I get there, fine. If not, they probably won't miss me, anyway.

My prayer: "Lord, continue to be with me, blessing me, helping me to be kind to others

Birdie Etchison, born in San Diego, California, raised in Portland, Oregon, now lives on the Long Beach Peninsula in the SW corner of Washington State. Birdie has had a variety of books published, including juvenile, nonfiction and fiction. She has been included in several anthologies and also writes articles and short stories. She sold a romance to Woman's World magazine and an article to Grit magazine, both publications she'd tried to sell to for years. Besides teaching at various conferences, Birdie was an instructor for Writer's Digest School for 22 years. She co-directed Writer's Weekend at the Beach, an annual gathering of writers for 17 years. As a past president of Oregon Christian Writers, Birdie is still active in that organization.

I'm Not Adequate

By Joi Copeland

As human beings, we have a great gift: the gift of comparing. It's true, isn't it? We compare our homes to others, we compare our cars, our jobs, our children, spouses, finances, etc. And you know what? We always come up lacking.

I, Joi, have four beautiful, smart, gifted, educated, and talented sisters. Each one of them can dance. Yet for some reason, the dancing gift passed right over me. I'm not as beautiful as they are, nor do I measure up to them in any way, shape, or form. Recently, Chris and I were able to attend a dinner and a session at World Venture's 75th anniversary. We were able to see most of our colleagues and talk with a few of them. I also had the privilege of talking with one of them while she is in Ireland. These women are gorgeous, godly, fantastic and truly amazing! There is no way I can ever measure up to them, either.

I have mastered the art of comparison, and let me tell you, I come up short every single time. I think some of you can relate, can't you? While we were traveling in June, I met with a dear friend and her family. I kept thinking, "There is no way I could ever be like her." And guess what? God doesn't want me to be. Over the course of June and into July, I kept having that recurring thought about people. It all boils down to this: I am not adequate to do God's work. I'll never measure up, I'll never be enough. I just won't be. And you know what? I don't have to be. Why? Why don't I have to be enough?

Because GOD IS ENOUGH. *"Now may the God of peace, who through the blood of the eternal covenant brought back from the dead our Lord Jesus, that great Shepherd of the sheep, [21] equip you with everything good for doing his will, and may he work in us what is pleasing to him, through Jesus Christ, to whom be glory for ever and ever. Amen"* Hebrews 13:20-21

I don't have to be enough, because God is. He is enough to fill me with the work He has called me to do. I'm not on this planet to do the same job as my sisters or my co-workers on the field or those who will be coming to the field. I am called to do the work God has set aside for me to do. Ephesians 4:12 continues in this line of thinking, "[2] for the equipping of the saints for the work of ministry, for the [e]edifying of the body of Christ"

Yet, I still find myself comparing, telling God I'm not strong enough to do what He is calling me to do. Then the words of Paul come rushing back to me, "And He said to me, "My grace is sufficient for you, for My strength is made perfect in **weakness**." *Therefore most gladly I will rather boast in my infirmities, that the power of Christ may rest upon me."* 2 Corinthians 12:9.

I don't have to be strong enough, God is. I don't have to be perfect, God is. I don't have to have it all together because God does. HE IS ENOUGH so I don't have to be.

This made started me thinking about the people in Ireland. Do they have these same struggles? Is this some of the reason why suicide and alcoholism run rampant in Ireland? I believe it to be so. I believe there are many people in Ireland who do not feel adequate. And who can tell them otherwise? With 72 towns with 5,000 people or more who do not have a gospel presence, how can they know the Truth? This is why I want to go to Ireland so badly. I want to share with these amazing people that they don't have to be enough. God is enough. They don't have to have it all together, God has it all together. The only thing they have to do is accept His great love for them. I'm not adequate to do it alone. And I don't have to be.

Turbulent Times

By Joi Copeland

Flying. There are some people who really enjoy the flying experience. They seem to feel at ease in the sky. They seem to like the thrill of defying gravity. Oh, and getting from one place to another in hours instead of months is always a draw to flying, right?

Not this gal. No ma'am. I do not like flying. Sure, I like the taking off and the landing portion of flying. But being in the air? Uh-uh. Nope. Not me. It's unsettling for me to be so high in the air with no place to go if something were to happen. I'm not too keen on the idea of having to use my pressure mask or flotation device.

Yet, the life of a missionary requires me to fly. We have to travel from state to state, giving our presentation, sharing with churches and pastors. And when God says it's time, we have to fly to Ireland and begin our ministry. It's par for the course. It's part of the job.

Just last week, we were in Portland, Maine. We then traveled to Vermont by car since it isn't too far to drive. Then we headed back to Maine to fly home to Denver, Colorado. To say our flights were turbulent free would be a lie. Especially our flight from Baltimore.

We were sitting on the plane before taking off when the pilot came out to suggest we use the bathroom now since we were going to experience pretty heavy turbulence, and he wasn't going to let the flight attendants up during time either.

Um, what? Say again? Turbulence. I despise turbulence. And here the pilot was telling us we were going to experience a lot of it. I wanted nothing more than to jump out of my seat, grab my luggage, and take a train home. That was my thought.

But that's not what happened. I stayed on the plane, we took off, we were rerouted, and still had turbulence. I spent a lot of time in prayer on that flight. Who am I kidding? On every flight. Philippians 4:6-7 (NKJ) states "**6** Be anxious for nothing, but in everything by prayer and supplication, with thanksgiving, let your requests be made known to God; **7** and the peace of God, which surpasses all understanding, will guard your hearts and minds through Christ Jesus." I spent a lot of time in prayer, thanking God for the opportunity to be in Maine and Vermont, asking Him to change my heart in regards to flying. I asked God for peace, His peace, no matter what happened.

And I saw beauty on that flight. I looked at the window and saw God's creation. It was amazing! I was reminded that yes, in life, I will have turbulence. John 16:33 NKJ *"These things I **have** spoken to **you**, that **in** Me **you** may **have** peace. **In** the **world you will have** tribulation; but be of good cheer, I **have** overcome the **world**."*

Jesus has overcome the world. Isn't that great news? No matter what turbulence comes your way, rest in the fact that Jesus has overcome the world!

Dear friends, as always, feel free to email me at booksbyjoi@copelandclan.com or find me on Facebook. I'd love to hear from you!

God bless you all!

In His Grip,

Joi Copeland

Phil. 4:6-8

National Suicide Prevention
1-800 273 8255

https://joicopeland.com/
https://www.facebook.com/BooksByJoiCopeland

Stuck in a Blackberry Bush

By June Foster

"Out of my distress I called on the Lord; the Lord answered me and set me free." Psalms 118:5

When my kids were young, my husband was in the army. When my daughter Kelly was about seven, we were stationed at Ft. Lewis, Washington. The area is surrounded by towering lush Douglas fir, sparkling lakes and streams, and blackberry bushes. Blackberry plants have sharp thorns, and it's easy to get scratched.

One day, my youngest daughter Susan ran into the house saying Kelly was caught in a blackberry bush. I rushed out to the edge of the forested area near our house on base. Sure enough, Kelly was held captive by the ferocious spikes. She had only wanted to taste one of the juicy berries that grew between the prickly spikes.

In no time, I helped Kelly get free. I had her take off her sweater which had mostly come in contact with the bush. Once she slipped out of that, she was free, and we eventually retrieved her sweater.

This morning I thought about how this is how we humans are. We get ourselves in the worst predicaments, but God, like a patient, loving Father, frees us from our calamities. He's our Father, and He's God.

Dear Lord, thank you for caring about us and loving us. Allow us to know You better and better. We are grateful for Your mighty power and love. You, who number all the hairs on our heads, You who said, "Look at the birds of the air; they do not sow or reap or store away in barns, and yet your heavenly Father feeds them. Are you not much more valuable than they?" You who died for us so we might live, we give You all glory and praise. Amen.

A Prayer for our Nation

Patterned After 11 Chronicles 7:14

By June Foster

Dear Lord,

I pray for Your people, including myself. We are in awe that You would choose to call us by Your great name. We are unworthy, yet You bestowed Your name upon us. Help us to remember we are but dust and that You are the God of gods and King of kings who has created all that exists. Help us to humble ourselves before You.

We seek You, for You alone are worthy. Only You can forgive our sins. Grant that we may turn from our inclinations to follow the world. How easy it is to want to fit in, but these worldly wrongs only stand between You and us. Allow us to walk away when faced with temptation. Living for You is more valuable than anything this world can offer.

Lord, You have promised that if we distance ourselves from godless ventures, you will hear our prayers and forgive our sins. We claim Your precious promise to heal our land, the United States of America, our homeland.

Amen.

11 Chronicles 7: 14

"If my people, who are called by my name, will

humble themselves and pray and seek my face and turn from their wicked ways, then I will hear from heaven, and I will forgive their sin and will heal their land."

Counting Blessings Instead of Sheep

By June Foster

I know most people my age have heard the song that admonishes us to count our blessings instead of sheep when we're having a hard time getting to sleep.

Tossing and turning some nights plagues everyone, no matter what the age. Our head hits the pillow and our thoughts cut loose like a bunch of marathon runners. Did I pay the electricity bill? What should I get my husband for his birthday? I only wrote one chapter instead of two today. We simply can't let go of the stressors of the day. And in the middle of the night, problems seem magnified and overwhelming. Internal thoughts hinder our sleep.

I looked up some techniques that psychologists suggest. One is imagine placing the thought on a leaf and tossing the leaf off in a stream, allowing it to float away. Another is don't go to bed until really sleepy, and go to bed at the same time every night.

But I found a strategy that benefits me every time. When I'm tossing, I heed the words of the old song about counting blessings. I know that sounds really simple, but when we thank God for our blessings and acknowledge that all good things come from Him, we can't help but

93

become relaxed and drowsy. Too, some of those blessings may fill our dreams.

James 1:17 *"Every good and perfect gift is from above, coming down from the Father of the heavenly lights, who does not change like shifting shadows."*

Proverbs 10:6a *"Blessings crown the head of the righteous."* That's a promise I want to embrace. Count your blessings and give thanks to the Lord.

Dear Lord, I pray for the readers of this little devotional. Allow them to take hold of Your Word which proclaims them to be Your children, ones You have declared righteous. Cover each with a blanket of peace, that they may be able to set aside the cares of this world and rest in You as they slumber. Amen.

Dealing With Poor Health

By June Foster

As I get older, I'm plagued with health issues, not unlike most of us. Aches and pains that weren't there before. Or more serious diseases that afflict our bodies. Unfortunately, we don't have to be older to have health problems. Illness strikes at every age. But there is a positive side to poor health, believe it or not.

When we're not able to carry on with daily tasks, when our bodies don't cooperate, we suddenly have time for reflection and become acutely aware of our finite nature. When I was younger, I thought I was invincible. No more.

In the opportunity to put life into perspective, we realize how much we need and depend on God and place our trust in the Almighty and not self. Yes, this is a tough subject, but I think some of us need to think about it.

Loved ones or our good health may be stripped away from us. But there is still One who will never leave or forsake us. We can hold on to this and be filled with joy. In Hebrews 13:5, God says, *"Never will I leave you; never will I forsake you."* That's a promise we can embrace.

Dear Lord, I pray for many of us who have

reached our twilight years. Allow us to continue to serve You until the day You call us home. Help us to remember that our bodies may be wasting away, but inwardly we are being renewed day by day. Though the aches and pains may not go away, teach us to keep our eyes on You and our reward in the next world to come. Amen.

Internet Problems

By June Foster

U p until last winter, my husband and I traveled full time in our RV. The lifestyle is an exciting adventure with plenty of opportunities to meet wonderful people and see the US. We experienced historical sites, national parks, and the beauty each state has to offer. However, one frustrating aspect of RVing is the variation in internet access. And any author can tell you how much we depend on the web.

In El Paso, I had one of the most frustrating experiences. I depended on my Sprint Air Card, which served me well in most locations. But not so in this city situated in the corner of western Texas. I wanted to believe the people at the Sprint store who said they had no idea why I couldn't get the internet, but it still didn't work. I had to give up any thought of visiting Facebook orTwitter, much less working with my critique group.

Looking back, I see the frustration and hopelessness that plagued me. The enemy probably delighted in my angst. But in the midst of the situation, the Lord reminded me to depend on Him alone and rest in His peace.

Remain in me, and I will remain in you. No branch can bear fruit by itself. It must remain in the vine. Neither can you bear fruit unless you remain in me. John 15:4

I wound up getting a lot done on my work-in-progress as well as learning to trust the Lord and enjoy His peace.

The situation helped me learn that above all, I can rely on Him. The internet was not the answer, but the Lord. *Trust in the Lord with all you heart and lean not on your own understanding. In all your ways acknowledge Him, and He will direct your paths. Proverbs 3: 5-6*

"You intended to harm me, but God intended it for good to accomplish what is now being done." *Genesis 50:20*

Dear Lord, please help us to trust in You and not in ourselves. When something goes wrong, remind us to seek you first and not pray as a last resort. Your ways are not our ways, and You possess all wisdom and knowledge. Help us to rest in You and Your mighty power. Amen.

Death of His Saints

By June Foster

I received the call. My 93-year-old aunt was nearing the time when the Lord would call her home. She'd been unconscious for a couple of days. I'd be sad that I wouldn't be able to talk to her on the phone any longer or take her out to lunch for her birthday again or hear her sweet laugh any longer.

Before she passed away, I considered how I could pray for her, and the Lord gave me a beautiful prayer. Any elderly person who's sick could benefit from this:

Lord, so fill (put in the person's name) with Your Holy Spirit, Your presence, and Your love that there is barely any room left for pain and disease.

I'll miss my aunt, but praise be to the Lord, she was a believer. We've talked about how we'll see each other again in the next life. If I'm sure of anything, I'm positive of the reality of Heaven.

Precious in the sight of the Lord is the death of His saints. Psalm 116:15

Good bye, Aunt Gina. I love you.
Virginia Mills 1909-2013

A Phone Call to God

By June Foster

Ring.
Ring.
"Hello. You've reached Jeremiah 33:3 and will be connected immediately with no waiting time to speak to God."

"Yes." I lowered my fist in a victory signal. "Hello, God."

"Good morning, my daughter. I love you, today."

"I love you, too, Lord. I was reading Ephesians 6:14 today about my breastplate of righteousness. I think mine has slipped. It's a bit dinted, and there are a few holes in it, too, where the devil's fiery darts attacked me."

"Yes. That happens. I seem to recall a few years back when the enemy was especially on your case. Right before you were going to teach that little class of ten fifth graders in VBS. The pastor had had an exasperating day, and you witnessed his conversation with the VBS director. You left before you could witness your pastor begging for forgiveness. You thought some impure and critical thoughts that day."

"Uh, oh. I remember. Yes, I lost some of my enthusiasm about VBS." I drew a long breath and blew it out. Surely God heard my frustrated sigh. "These days, Lord, I find my thoughts sliding into judgmental and selfish notions. I'm always asking what's in it for me. I don't like my attitude, but the thoughts keep coming. Can I put in an order for a new breast plate?"

A soft chuckle. "Your old one is perfect because I made it. If anyone is in Christ, the new creation has come: The old has gone. Don't fear, my child. In this world you will have trouble. But take heart. I have overcome the world. "

Again, I exhaled a long breath. "Thank you, Lord, my God and my Savior." I hung up and read Ephesians 6: 14 one more time.

"Stand firm then, with the belt of truth buckled around your waist, with the breastplate of righteousness in place.":

Dear Lord, I've lived in this world long enough to know Your people are in a spiritual battle, yet You have not left us as orphans but provided weapons of warfare. Help me each day to seek truth in Your holy word and arm myself with the breastplate of righteousness. Thank you that You are greater than our enemy. I love you. Amen."

Choices

By June Foster

Sometimes I try to imagine what God is like. My finite mind can't comprehend even a fraction of His attributes. *"As the heavens are higher than the earth, so are my ways higher than your ways and my thoughts than your thoughts."* Isaiah 55:9 How far are the heavens from the earth? Even from here to the moon is mind boggling.

I like to imagine God creating the earth, the heavens, and everything there is. "In the beginning God created the heavens and the earth." He formed all that is from nothing. Think about the intricate workings of the eye—or the how the ear hears—or how the tide goes in and out. As we used to say, it blows my mind.

He has power over everything—the weather, angels and demons, the course of history. Yet one fact, astounds me. God allows man free will to make his own choices. He didn't have to permit that. Could our own free will be responsible for murder, theft, adultery, abortion, homosexuality? The list could go on.

I'm in awe of a powerful God who would let me make my own choices. I choose to serve and please our awesome Creator.

"For whatever a man sows, that he will also reap. For he who sows to his flesh will of the flesh reap corruption, but he who sows to the Spirit will of the

Spirit reap everlasting life." Galatians 6:7-8

Dear Lord, help me each day to make wise choices. Instruct me from Your word and place your will in my heart so I may do and say those things that glorify Your name. Amen.

A Field of Daisies

By June Foster

As everyone knows, while we're on this earth, no one escapes the negatives of life. Christians included.

Too, the more years we live, the more time for the effects of unpleasant and stressful issues to accumulate and weigh us down. I used to think that when I got older, I could deal with problems more easily. It didn't work that way.

But wait. What about Jesus' words where he says, *"Cast all your burdens on me because I care for you."*

What does that look like? I believe it means to tell Him about our concerns, pray for those involved, and set aside the emotional pain, enjoying the confidence that comes from knowing the Lord is in charge. Too bad I didn't learn that when I was in my thirties or forties.

I have to admit. I inherited my melancholy nature from my father. But that's no excuse. I use to worry about people and situations in my life I had no control over. When I prayed, I'd crawl in an emotional hole, allowing the burden to become heavier and heavier.

I've discovered a wonderful way to pray these days. I'm sure many others already do this. As I pray, I visualize the concern or the person then I see the cross of Christ. I picture myself laying the burden, perhaps in the form of a big box or bundle, down in front of the cross, enjoying the confidence that God is in charge and not me. Then I run to a field of daisies, frolicking and praising the Lord.

"Cast your burden on the Lord and he will sustain you; he will never permit the righteous to be moved." Psalm 55:22

Dear Lord, thank You that You are a mighty God, and You love me. You want the best for Your people and You have promised to sustain us. Help me to avail myself of your offer to carry our burdens. Amen."

Forgiveness

By June Foster

Forgiveness is a popular subject among Christians and in devotionals. It's easy to talk about but not so simple to do. But for the Christian to forgive is vital. In fact, God may not forgive us of our wrongdoings, if we can't forgive others.

"If you forgive others the wrongs they have done to you, your Father in heaven will also forgive you. But if you do not forgive others, then your Father will not forgive the wrongs you have done." Matthew 6:14-15

Wow. That's a pretty powerful statement. But God's word is truth, so we better take it to heart.

"But, God, you don't understand," I'm tempted to say sometimes. "That person told a lie which cost me my job. He hates me and has no compassion on me. Besides he's not a Christian."

Does that change God's mind? I don't think so.

"Well, God. What about my alcoholic husband who left me to raise our three children? Am I supposed to forgive him? He doesn't deserve it."

Forgiveness is way harder than we think, but ponder this. On the cross, Jesus said "Forgive them for they don't know what they're doing." The Roman army pierced Jesus' hands and feet with nails, yet he didn't hold it against them.

All of us are like sheep and have gone astray. None

STREAMS OF JOY

of us is without sin, but did God forgive you when you sought salvation? Forgiveness is like God's grace— letting go of someone's wrongdoing against you. The Bible commands us to be more like Jesus.

Do we deserve forgiveness? The question has an obvious answer. No. So if God can forgive us, can't we forgive another?

"Be kind to one another, tenderhearted, forgiving one another, as God in Christ forgave you." Ephesians 4:32

Dear Lord, today I choose to forgive those who've hurt me, wronged me, and let me down. I cannot do it in my own strength. In fact, I don't even feel like forgiving, but I know through You I can pardon that person who harmed me. I choose to do it by faith. Today I have been set free from the bitterness that has gripped me. In Jesus name. Amen.

God is Our Refuge

By June Foster

Since moving to Alabama, I've found that wind or rain storms pop up out of nowhere. All of a sudden it's not comfortable outdoors, and I seek the shelter of my house. My comfy brick home is a refuge from straight-line winds and pelting downpours. In the winter, I remain toasty warm when the out-of-doors is getting a blanket of snow. Thank God for my safe and secure dwelling place.

However, my soul and spirit need a refuge as well—a safe harbor. God protects me from the storms of life—bitterness, doubt, fear, disappointment, loneliness. I'm not saying I never experience these punishing emotions, but when I do, I run to the Lord.

The book of Psalms contains a wealth of scriptures about how God is our refuge. 71:7 says, "*But you are my strong refuge.*" 94:22 assures us, "*But the Lord has become my fortress, and my God, the rock in whom I take refuge.*" In 142: 5, David calls out, "*I cry to you, O Lord; I say, 'You are my refuge, my portion in the land of the living.'*"

Want more like these? Look up refuge in your concordance. You'll find enough to satisfy your soul.

No matter where we are in life, we need God—our refuge. On occasion I even picture myself in the throne room, next to Jesus or in His loving arms. Try it sometime.

Dear Lord, teach me to remember I can run to You. You are my high tower and place of safety. The world has no control over me. You are almighty and are faithful. Amen.

Grace

By June Foster

G race. We in the Christian community hear that word a lot. *"For it is by grace you have been saved, through faith, and this is not from yourselves, it is the gift of God."* Ephesians 2:8

There is absolutely nothing you can do to make yourself acceptable to stand in the presence of God. No amount of good works will be sufficient. It's one of the most precious gifts Christians can possess.

But do we really understand grace? When I tell someone outside the faith about God's grace, they generally scoff and say it's too easy. Why wouldn't God require us to do more to get right with Him? It's a challenging question since we tend to want to control our lives and strive for what we need and want.

I believe even Christians struggle with the concept of grace. I know that I do. Frequently I discover an ugly thought lurking in my head. Or, a comment that speaks ill of someone else erupts from my mouth without permission. Or I eat that extra dessert I didn't need then later I ask myself why.

Each time, I receive that gentle reminder from the Holy Spirit that my thoughts or deeds are sinful, He allows me to confess and ask forgiveness. But that seems to happen daily, hourly. Does God really forgive us that many times?

Yep. His grace is sufficient for us.

I can only thank and praise Him for his powerful grace working in my life.

"But he said to me, 'My grace is sufficient for you, for my power is made perfect in weakness.'" 11 Corinthians 12:9

Dear Lord, when I am tempted to rely on my own merits or good deeds, remind me that it is only by Your grace that I am pleasing to You. I thank You that it's not about me, but all about you. Amen.

The Parable of the Robin

One spring a robin pecked incessantly on our dining room window. It almost drove me crazy. I read on the internet that they are fighting the imaginary bird they see reflected there. I figure that poor bird must have damaged his beak and become exhausted by the end of the day.

The problem sparked a thought in my mind. The bird fought an unnecessary battle. He thought there was danger to his nest, but in reality he only exerted unneeded energy.

The poor creature kept striving yet made no progress in accomplishing anything. How often are we like that bird, expending unfruitful effort when we could better utilize our time in other ways. I know, I certainly do. So what's the answer?

This scripture came to mind. Psalm 46:10. *"Be still, and know that I am God."* God knows everything about us and has a perfect plan, if we will but quiet ourselves and listen.

John 10 speaks of the shepherd of our souls. *"I am the good shepherd."* Allow Him to lead.

Dear Lord, help me to make prudent decisions and practice the wisdom that's available if we only ask You. I pray that You will help me spend my time fruitfully doing those things that glorify You and Your kingdom and not on unnecessary or unwise endeavors. Amen.

Half full vs. half empty

We've all heard the half empty, half full discussion. I'll be honest. I have to force myself to perceive the glass as half full much of the time. My normal inclination is to see the dreary side of things. I guess that's my old melancholy nature I inherited from somewhere.

But I've received an inheritance much more important than the genes of my ancestors. 1Peter1:3-4 say: *"Praise be to the God and Father of our Lord Jesus Christ! In his great mercy he has given us new birth into a living hope through the resurrection of Jesus Christ from the dead, and into an inheritance that can never perish, spoil or fade—kept in heaven for you."* As Christians, we now look forward to a family heritage in the eternal city of God.

It's easy to see the glass half full with this perspective. Sure life has disappointments, pain, and hardship, the half empty glass. But look what's in store for us in the future. I fix my eyes on the half full glass of the present and praise my God for his blessings. My day is filled with joy when I'm able to see life in this manner.

Once when we were RVing, I looked out the

window. I saw the perfect example. The first picture was in the foreground—an ugly tool shed. But beyond I saw a grassy knoll.

"Let us fix our eyes on Jesus, the author and perfecter of our faith," and we'll never see the glass half empty again.

Dear Lord, help us to fix our eyes on things above and not the things of this world. The world will pass away but You are with us for all eternity. Please give us this heavenly perspective. Amen.

Life After Life

By June Foster

I tend to dread hearing about friends and family my own age that have passed on, but the reality of the next life should bring great joy. And I suppose it's a subject a person of any age might think about.

It makes no sense to say that when this life is over, we will remain forever unaware, unconscious, and completely dead under the earth. What about our minds that wonder, think, explore— feelings that experience a gamut of emotions, and the spirit within that seeks to find its Maker? Does all that come to an end when our frame enters the grave? I don't believe we possess all those marvelous components for them to cease to exist.

Where did I get these ideas from? A good source. The Bible says we are aliens and strangers in this world. – 1Peter 2:11. When I lived in Germany for three years, I was an alien citizen in that country. Where was my true earthly citizenship? The United States of America. So if I'm an alien in this world, where is my real home?

When Jesus left this earth, He referred to the next life when he said that in His father's house were many rooms, and He was going there to prepare a place for me and every other Christian. John 14:2. Revelation 21 tells us that the dwelling place of God will be with men. It's an existence where there are no more tears, death, crying or pain. In fact, He's making it brand new. That sounds like Heaven to me.

"For God so loved the world that he gave his one and only Son, that whoever believes in him shall not perish but have eternal life." John 3:16

Dear Lord, please grant me a heavenly perspective as I travel through this life. Help me to continually be aware of and rejoice in the truth of my eternal destination— the perfect life that awaits.

One Day Jesus

L ast week I sat down to read my Daily Bread devotional. The scripture began in Luke 11. I started reading verse one. "One day Jesus..." I couldn't read any farther. The words "one day Jesus" continue to reverberate in my mind. I said the words over and over.

Verse one of Luke 11 precedes the verses where Jesus teaches his disciples how to pray. Yet I couldn't get past the simple meaning I found in those three words. Jesus came to earth from heaven dwelling in time and space. He walked the earth for approximately 12,045 days. On one of those days, he taught his disciples to pray. On many the other days, he taught people how to live and love each other. And on the final day, he made the supreme sacrifice giving his life for all mankind.

The reality of the message hit me square in the middle of my heart. One day we will see Jesus face to face. One day we'll live in His presence for all eternity. One day, a day will never end. One day Jesus. Halleluiah.

"One day Jesus was praying in a certain place. When he finished, one of his disciples said to him, 'Lord, teach us to pray, just a John taught his disciples.'" Luke 11:1

Dear Lord, I thank You for the reality of Jesus Christ, our Savior. You sent Him to this earth for a very specific purpose and out of Your love. Through Him and Him alone can we receive forgiveness of sins and join You someday in heaven. Amen.

Would you like to keep up with June's latest releases and what's going on in her life? Sign up at June's website.

I always love to hear from readers. Write me at junefoster11@gmail.com

Find me on the web at:

Amazon Author page

Twitter

Facebook

Goodreads

May the Lord richly bless you.

A Good Light

By Bonnie Engstrom

My eyes are getting older and my vision dimmer. Even with my new reading glasses, an expensive prescription, not to mention the costly designer frames, words sometimes blur, and letters look like they are outlined in downy fuzz.

A good reading light – that's what I need. Unfortunately, most are expensive, and many are ugly. I can't seem to find one I like that coordinates with my living room decor at a price I can afford.

Good light is important, even valuable. But, one light is invaluable. God's. No value can be put on it. It is truly priceless.

In John 8:12, Jesus said, *"I am the light of the world. Whoever follows me will never walk in darkness, but will have the light of life."* What a promise.

I have a lot of friends who wear glasses. Some, like me, take them on and off frequently. For some, it's a nervous habit. For others they're "on" for reading and driving and watching TV and "off" for talking over coffee. It depends on their vision perspective, whether near-sighted or far-sighted. Although I definitely need my glasses for reading and writing, I also need them for thinking. I almost never use them for driving, unless I'm at an intersection where I can't read the street sign. I don't want to become *too* dependent on them. I suppose it's a vanity thing.

When Christ claimed to be "the light of the world" it wasn't a vain statement. He didn't take the promise "on" and "off" ever. He spoke not out of nervous habit, but as the Son of God, the Anointed One. His words were not frivolous, not to be taken lightly, and not to be claimed only when we need to read a street sign. His street signs were always clear, glowing in big bold letters for all to read easily.

I finally found my perfect lamp online, and at a reasonable price. Hubby spent an unreasonable time putting it together, reading the instructions that were written in broken English. Unfortunately, there are scratches on the base and the fake glass over the bulb has a small crack. He discouraged me from returning it. After all, no one would see the base tucked under the skirt of the chair, and the crack was hardly visible. Besides, even if he could figure out how to take apart the numerous pieces and put them back in the packing box's indentations, we'd have to pay the return postage and wait another ten days for a replacement. He convinced me.

I read gratefully under the lamp's light each night.

Sometimes as I read, knowing the crack and scratches are there, they bother me. Then I think about all the scratches and cracks I have on me, on my heart. The scratches that come out of my mouth when I'm not allowing God's light to shine in me; the sinful cracks in my past.

Jesus either ignores those or has repaired them. He has bathed me in His light. He took all those scratches and cracks upon Himself when He hung on the cross.

No matter how dim my vision becomes, if I look up to the Savior, I will always be walking and reading and driving in the light.

Thank you, Heavenly Father for shining Your light on the world, and especially on me. Please remind me when I see downy fuzz around the letters of my life that the softness is Your hand upon me guiding me on the path you want me to take. Thank you for not disassembling me and sending me back, but for keeping me – scratches and cracks and all.

A Hungry Dog

By Bonnie Engstrom

We have the cutest little dog. Jake is a Min-Pin, a Miniature Pinscher, small in stature, big in appetite. Although originally the standard reddish-brown, designated red, instead of the more common black and brown, he's almost fifteen and, like his earthly "daddy," has a white-frosted snout. There is a lot of silly press about how dogs and their owners tend to look alike. It's true my dear husband's beard is now gray, and he has a longish nose, like Jake. Maybe it's not so silly.

Jake's ears were never clipped, thankfully, and they make him resemble a forest deer. One ear, though, flops giving him a quizzical look. I'm sure he uses the expression it gives him to melt our hearts. One ear sticking straight up to Heaven, the other with its corner bent and his head cocked to one side are hard to resist. Not to mention his "sit." The only accolade he got from his training classes was "The Best Sit." Of course, any idiot, myself included, could surmise he did it for the ensuing treat.

Even a dozen years later when I'm the one taking him for his constitutional I try to reinforce the training. He definitely remembers "sit." But, we've had our moments with "stay" while I walk away from him in the sitting position; "leave it" when he's supposed to abandon a smell or some chicken bones thrown onto the sidewalk. He does best when greeting other dogs, unless they are Golden Retrievers. He always gets a treat for being a "good boy," but he always, yes always, lunges at the throats of Goldens.

We adopted Jake from a pet store that held doggie adoptions every weekend. That weekend he was the only tiny dog among a dozen large ones. He had been in doggie foster care after running away twice and being abandoned. We never thought to ask, but we believe he was the

little guy and the woman who fostered him had a lot of Goldens, who probably pushed him away from food.

We'll never know, not until Jake can communicate in English.

What we do know is Jake is always hungry. He can be upstairs and hear me open the refrigerator; he can be snuggled in his blankie (a Min-Pin thing) and hear me open a zip-lock bag. He is instantly at my feet. He will lick a paper plate with only a few crumbs left on it.

We've asked the vet, and he says it's a Min-Pin trait.

Are you always "hungry?" Do you feel as if you need more? More sustenance, more support in your daily life. I don't mean more actual food, although that may be the case for some. I do mean the need to always be fed with God's Word.

It's so simple, too simple; we often forget that the Bible is food. For our hearts, our brains and our struggle with daily living.

Some biblical scholars say you shouldn't just open God's word randomly. Others proclaim that doing so will direct you to the very passage you need to read. I've done both. Sometimes the passage is exactly what I needed to confirm and be affirmed. Other times, I wonder why the book flipped open in James or, horrors, Job. At first the words didn't speak to my need. But, trying to be obedient I read a few lines. Wow! I found not only couldn't I stop reading, but the words and the situation spoke to me – for my need, that day, that moment.

Like Jake I am always hungry. Sometimes my stomach growls, other times my heart does. If your heart growls, or even your stomach, open God's plan for your life. Don't be like Jake always craving food. Don't be hungry. Lift up that heavy tome and open it, randomly. Then open your heart to the words.

Thank you, Jesus, for your precious, live-giving words of wisdom and support. Please remind me and encourage me to open and read the Book of Life, the life instructions, you have given me. Please feed me with your words. Fill my belly, my brain and my heart. – Bonnie Engstrom

Pay Attention

By Bonnie Engstrom

He's following too close.

The black SUV behind me was so close I could see the drivers face in my rearview mirror. I'd put my right turn signal on at least a block before. Either he didn't see it because he wasn't paying attention, or he was "cowboy driver" testing fate.

Thankfully, as I slowed down for the turn, he must have eased on his throttle. Still, he was close enough if I'd had to stop suddenly, there would have been a rear-ender collision.

Turning onto the side street I checked the rearview mirror again and saw the blur of his car as it sped past. I whispered a quiet "Thank you, Lord" and relaxed my hands on the wheel.

Then I prayed that God would guide him so he wouldn't hurt anyone, himself included. I did ask the Lord to maybe give him a little scare, a reminder to drive more safely. Nothing major, just something to frighten him enough to be a more cautious driver.

Do you ever feel like you're being dogged, followed too closely by circumstances and people in your life? Maybe you have no breathing room from your spouse or your kids or friends. Everyone wants a piece of you. You are interrupted during your morning devotions, although kindly, by your spouse chatting, or a phone call from a child who needs advice. You feel as if you're always watching your back; you check the caller I.D. before answering the phone. It's your dearest friend, your sister in Christ. You decide to call her back, later. She doesn't leave a message, so you wonder, and worry. Does she have an emergency, or does she just want to chat?

Guilt takes over, and you close your book of devotions setting it and your Bible aside. You pour another cup of decaf Hazelnut coffee, stir in a lot of cream and dial.

Thank heavens she just wanted to chat, to share a small victory she had with a child in her Sunday School class. It really was a cute moment for her, and you laugh together.

You close your eyes and thank the good Lord you have such a dear friend. You feel blessed. Tomorrow you vow you will call her, just for no reason at all. Just to chat.

Thank you, Lord, for special friends, for godly sisters. Help me to appreciate my friends more and be there for their needs, their trials and their triumphs. Make me a better friend, a friend who is sensitive and caring and who is willing to take time from a busy day to listen.

Scavenger Hunt

By Bonnie Engstrom

Yea! Wee!" The children held up their lists waving them in the air above their heads. They clasped hands with their game partners and squirmed impatiently for the whistle to blow.

"I love scavenger hunts!" A freckle-faced child grinned and her ponytail swayed as she jiggled on bouncing feet. I blew the whistle and the pre-teens scurried for the door, each holding a grocery bag. The hunt was on. As I set the kitchen timer for thirty minutes I laughed, thinking how much they resembled a mini-thundering herd.

The hardest item on their list was a gold paper clip. Mmm, I wondered if any neighbors owned one. I was pretty sure the cotton ball, Q-tip and even birdseed would be easily acquired. Probably also page twelve of the daily paper. I'd thrown that in because today was my daughter's twelfth birthday. I thought the list was a success remembering the expressions of delight on twelve faces. But, the gold-colored paper clip would surely be a challenge. Probably every neighbor on our block had some of the more common silver-colored ones. Was I the only person with a gold-colored one?

The children finally returned. They had been instructed to ask at each house what the time was. When it was five minutes before the hour they were to hustle back. (I discovered twelve-year-olds are good at following instructions.) Four of the six teams found everything – except the gold paper clip. My party-planner mother's guilt kicked in. Had I given them an impossible task? I was reminded of my daughter's favorite book when she was three, *It's Not Fair!* Maybe it wasn't fair, but sometimes life isn't. Had I presented them with an honest disappointment they'd soon forget, or had I taken away the fun of the game?

Life is full of challenges, small every day hiccups and giant life-changing tragedies. The lack of a gold paper clip seemed to be no more than a hiccup. The children soon forgot their disappointment as I passed out appropriate prizes. The gooey birthday cake was a catalyst for preteen memory loss. That is until the birthday girl announced around a mouthful of frosting, "My mom has gold paper clips. I remember 'cause I gave them to her for Christmas." Uh, oh. I felt heat creep into my cheeks.

"Mom, we could have gotten them from you." I stood accused and striding to my desk I opened a drawer. I handed each child a gold paper clip while pointing out to get one from me during the scavenger hunt wouldn't have been fair.

"Life isn't always fair, kiddos. Besides, it's possible one of the neighbors could have had one. Now that you each have your own, take it home to remind you of the party and the game."

The kids dropped the clip into their favor bags, except one boy who clipped it on his shirt pocket like a badge.

Do you feel like you're missing that one piece of gold, the most special ingredient in your life's favor bag? God said all you have to do is ask and your bag will be full, in fact filled to overflowing. When you do you'll be wearing His badge of glory. Accept His offering of gold and clip it on.

Thank you, Lord, that I don't have to hunt for You and for completing my favor bag with a badge of gold. May I wear it proudly to proclaim my love for You and Yours for me.

A Tree for All Seasons

By Bonnie Engstrom

I turned off the Christmas tree lights for the last time tonight. As I clicked the button I knew I'd miss the soft glow in the corner of the room while I read my novel before bed. A fleeting thought came then, almost as if my heart spoke to me. Why not, why couldn't I, have the tree stay there?

At Easter it could be decorated with egg ornaments and hand-crotched crosses to signify Christ's sacrifice on the cross; in Fall with nuts and tiny renditions of woodsy creatures - squirrels, chipmunks, brilliantly colored birds, rabbits and even bears. Spring would glorify it with branches of yellow forsythia blossoms, silk tulips and callas from the craft store, perhaps a hummingbird or two with sparkling green throats. Each and every holiday would be celebrated on the tree. Flags for Memorial Day, Fourth of July (maybe sparklers, too) and Veterans Day.

Each child and grandchild's birthdays would be acknowledged by photos of parties and pictures of the child from birth to the current year. Anniversaries of marriage and those who left us to live with the Lord would be announced with photos and special sayings. There would even be a special week for pets. I'm sure the ASPCA could oblige with sayings and photos. I have some special ones of my beloved pet friends from now (Hi, Jake!) and many years past.

How about other celebrations? Promotions, new jobs, new homes, milestones in life.

I love this idea. Yet, I have to admit it would be a lot of work on my part. Guess I'd be the one to assemble all the ornaments and decorate the tree.

Maybe it's easier to just bundle it up in its box and put it in storage for another year.

What a sad commentary on our busy lives.

Thank You, Lord, for wonderful and lasting memories. Please help me hang them on the tree of my heart and never forget how you've blessed me. Remind me at every blessing, every holiday – personal and national – to praise You for the gift of Your love.

Those Pesky Tasks

By Bonnie Engstrom

I hate folding laundry, especially socks, especially my husband's. I admit his are easier to figure out than mine. His are either gray or white with yellow heels and toes, sometimes beige. The only socks I wear are all black for donning my boots, so it's a challenge to pair the correct black socks with each other – ridges or not.

Another task I do with diligence, but would rather not have to, is emptying the dishwasher. Sometimes I forget where a strainer goes, or a scraper. Usually my role is to load the dreaded thing. I have a friend who says she's never known anyone who could load a dishwasher like me. Guess that's a compliment about my organizational skills. I do usually manage to wiggle everything in and still have each thing come out clean. It's a gift.

Today in church our pastor's message was about committing to try to be like Christ. That is so hard. Does it mean I have to give up every sinful thing? Try harder to not grumble over daily tasks? Not complain, mumbling, when it's my turn to walk the dog or turn off the lights before going to bed, or even make the bed?

I don't remember Christ mumbling or complaining about tasks set before Him. Like healing the sick or feeding the five thousand, or turning water into wine. He only said, you "… will walk with me."

"They will walk with me, dressed in white, for they are worthy." Revelation 3:4 (NIV)

Are you up to that task, to walk with Him? Can you imagine Him holding your hand, leading you, even helping you fold the laundry? You may not be able to do the miracles He did, but each task you undertake today is a small accomplishment. The very fact you have arms to fold the clothes and fingers to turn off the lights at night proclaims you as a walking miracle.

If you have no arms, literally, you can still honor the Lord, for you are a miracle of His love and grace. You have survived whatever presented you with that situation, whether birth or war or accident. You are equal to His tasks, the daily ones He has graciously given you to perform in His name.

Rejoice in the Lord, for He has given us daily tasks to remind us we are whole in Him.

Please, Father, let me feel Your presence as I perform the tasks You have set before me each day. Remind me to rejoice that I can do everything You ask and require with Your help. I praise You for giving me the strength and encouragement to fulfill Your wishes for my day.

Bonnie and her husband, Dave, have four grandchildren in Arizona a few miles from them. Three are girls, one of which is a twin with a boy who constantly endures teasing and giggling. Fortunately, Grandpa Dave spends special guy time with him to relieve him of girly talk and share Chick-fil-A.

The other two boys live in Costa Rica - Pura Vida! - with their father who has taught them to surf, skateboard and fish for their dinners. All six children, even though separated by continents, are very close and get together at least twice a year in either Costa Rica or Arizona where the two beach boys have to wear shoes!

Bonnie and Dave believe family is all. They feel very blessed to have grandchildren nearby, even though it often interrupts their schedule.

Bonnie is a long time member of American Christian Fiction Writers and a member of Christian Writers of the West in Arizona. She is a Pro Member of Romance Writers of America. She began her fiction writing career in California as a member of The Orange County Christian Writers Fellowship. She wrote the weekly education columns for two newspapers, The Newport Ensign and the Costa Mesa News. These organizations and the hundreds of newsletters she produced as a five time PTA president helped to hone her writing skills. The impetus for her writing was when she was the editor of her high school newspaper and wrote a weekly column for a local community paper, The Penn Hills Progress, too many years ago to mention. (Hint: She was only seventeen.)

She loves to connect with her readers. Her email address is bengstrom@hotmail.com. Be sure to put BOOK in the subject line. She would love to chat with you and answer any questions.

Visit her website http://www.bonnieengstrom.com (where you can see all those grandchildren) and link up with her on Facebook at https://www.facebook.com/bonnieengstromauthor/. To see all of her books go to http://bit.ly/2NgOiyd.

He Was Always There

By Teresa Ives Lilly

(Be strong and of a good courage, fear not, nor be afraid of them: for the LORD thy God, he it is that doth go with thee; he will not fail thee, nor forsake thee Joshua 1:9

A s a child, the one thing I remember most about my father is that he was always there. Every night after work, he was there, whenever I needed a ride he was there, if I wanted to come home from a slumber party at three o'clock in the morning he was there, when I needed money for college he was there and when we thought we might lose my mother he was there. The hardest thing I've ever had to face in life is the fact that now that my father has passed away, he is not there anymore. I can't see him, speak to him, ask him for help or tell him I love him. I will not ever forget the major impact he had on my family by always being there: A tower of strength.

My father was just a small reflection of what God is like. God is always there. When I sinned He was there, when I asked for forgiveness He was there, when I needed healing for my children he was there, when I needed to know that my father was really in Heaven He was there, and every day as I walk through life, He is there. God is the true tower of strength in life. (*II Samuel*

22:33 God is my strength and power.)

God has no intention of not being there. He has promised that He will always be there for us and never forsake us. *(Be strong and of a good courage, fear not, nor be afraid of them: for the LORD thy God, he it is that doth go with thee; he will not fail thee, nor forsake thee DE 31:6)*

Since God has determined to always be there, we in turn should do the same for Him. When He wakes you in the morning, be there, when he shows you someone who needs prayer, be there, when He whispers new challenges in your heart be there and when He calls you to heaven be there. You can see Him in the beauty of the world, you can speak to Him in prayer, you can get help from Him in the Word and you can tell Him every day that you love Him. Being there for God is the greatest way to assure yourself of a good life. Following His plans for your life will cause you to be strong. With His strength your way will be made perfect. *(II Samuel 22:33God is my strength and power: And he maketh my way perfect)*

I can name at least a hundred times in my life when I knew beyond a shadow of a doubt that God was there. Miracles in my home and family will always stand out as great reminders of His presence. Every day I know He is there, by the small soft voice that whispers to me, by the life I feel in my heart when I read His word or sing songs to Him. I can never doubt His presence. There are times though, when I think He can doubt mine. Times I have been too busy to read His word, or do His will, or help my neighbor or a stranger. Many times, when I'm sure God didn't think I was there.

Today, let us all dedicate ourselves to being there for God. If you have never made a commitment to Him, do it today. If you have not obeyed Him before, do it today. Think of all the times He has been there for you and choose this day to be there for God.

When I grow old, I will whisper to every person who can hear me:

He was always there!

Dear God: Help me to recognize your presence in my life today and every day. Let me be able to look at all my circumstances and say…. God was always there. Amen.

Teresa Ives Lilly loves to write Christian Fiction. In general, she writes novella length romance, but has been known to write a mystery or two and full-length novels.

Her novel, "Orphan Train Bride" quickly went to number one on Amazon's best seller list and stayed in the top ten for two weeks when first published.

She has participated in many novella collections, which have also been on the Amazon's bestseller list.

Teresa would love to hear from her readers. Readers can follow Teresa at www.teresalilly.wordpress.com

Teresa is always thankful for positive reviews left on Amazon for her books.

Teresa resides in San Antonio, Texas

A Soft Answer

By Gail Gaymer Martin

When I worked years ago as a guidance counselor, parents occasionally entered my office angry and frustrated. They came looking for someone to blame their problems. One day an angry father charged into my office, blaming the teachers and me for his daughter's problems. I could have returned his anger, but as I looked at this man towering above my desk with doubled fists, I saw in his eyes futility and fear. Here was a parent who did not know how to help his daughter with her problems.

"I don't blame you for feeling frustrated," I said softly. "Please have a seat, and let's see how we can work together to solve some of these problems."

He looked at me in surprise and, then, sat down quietly. "Thank you," he said. "Could I have a pencil and paper? I'd like to make some notes." Instead of sitting in the chair, he knelt on the floor in front of my desk and jotted ideas that we developed.

My fellow male counselor, concerned about the angry father, paced outside my office, and when the father left, he darted into the room. "How did you do that?" he asked. "He was so angry and then you had him on his knees."

"It wasn't me," I said, chuckling to myself. "It was God. I remembered the Lord's words to let forgiveness and love respond to anger." Remember *Proverbs 15:1 (NIV) A gentle answer turns away wrath, but a harsh word stirs up anger.*

Heavenly Father, when I open my mouth to respond to others who make us angry, help me remember that you have taught us that kindness is greater than malice. Let our response show your grace and love. In Jesus name, Amen

Faith of a Child

By Gail Gaymer Martin

I tell you the truth, anyone who will not receive the kingdom of God like a little child will never enter it. Mark 10: 15 (NIV)

Occasionally on Sunday morning the children's Sunday school choir sings during the worship service. I enjoy watching the wiggling, smiling children with their scrubbed faces, ruffled dresses, and little-men shirts. They sing with such joy and abandon. I hear their sweet voices singing, *Jesus Loves Me*, with confidence and assurance. Children listen to Bible stories with trust, faith, and innocence. They believe God's Word without challenge—without needing proof. It is a faith to be modeled after. As an adult I want proof. I need to see all the facts and analyze the information. I am skeptical and wary. Yet, Jesus has told us that all people must come to Him as a child, for we are the children of our Heavenly Father.

In 1 Corinthians, God explains why we do not understand all things. It is as if we are looking in a mirror, seeing only a reflection of God and of things to come. Someday we shall see God face to face. It is then that we will fully understand. If I model myself after the children, believing in God's Word without question, singing psalms and hymns with joy, and trusting in

God's promises, I will also worship and testify with abandon and delight, as Jesus has commanded.

Heavenly Father, so often we question your Word, question your promises and question you, seeing you only as a story someone one told because we are looking for proof and not looking at faith. Open our eyes, Lord to your truth and love. Let us stop searching for proof, but see the truth in the order of the universe, the beauty of the earth, the guidance that comes from somewhere beyond our being, and help us to hang on our childhood song, Jesus loves me this I know. In Jesus name, Amen

Finding the Key

by Gail Gaymer Martin

My aunt was one of those forgetful people you read about in funny stories. Finding the iron in the refrigerator or the milk sitting in a closet was not uncommon. Life was always one unexpected thing with Aunt Julia.

One day when we stopped by for a visit, she wasn't home, but being a hospitable lady, she left a note on the door. "The key is under the mat." I'm sure every burglar in town would thank Aunt Julia, but her note teaches a wonderful lesson.

God leaves the key under the mat for us every day. All he asks is for us to use it—listen to His word and trust in Him. But we aren't very trustful. Instead, we try to handle everything by ourselves and we don't rely on God. We're too busy patching things together when God could make them new again. But that takes faith and trust. I imagine Aunt Julia always found her milk and iron eventually. And I know many guests enjoyed her hospitality, even when she wasn't home.

In the same way, God's door is always open, and he is always home for us. Remember Jesus's words, *"Knock and the door will be opened for you."*

Dear Lord, help us to spend part of our day with you. You have provided us with your Word in the

form of the Bible, and you have promised to be with us and hear our prayers. You provide people in our lives to remind us of your love and promises. Help us to open the doors to all that you have provide us until the day we meet you face to face. In Jesus name, Amen

Forgiveness in Both Directions

by Gail Gaymer Martin

One day a bouquet of flowers arrived from a florist. When I opened the attached card, I was startled. The flowers were not from my husband but an old friend I hadn't seen in many years, a friend that I hadn't forgiven for her hurtful and thoughtless actions.

I'd always considered myself a forgiving person, but somehow the hurt I'd felt those many years early dwelt in my mind and heart. Our friendship had ended until the day the flowers arrived at my door.

But it wasn't the flowers that healed the wounds and made our friendship whole again. The blessing was the note attached to the bouquet. She reflected on the hurt she'd caused and asked for forgiveness.

My hard heart melted to tears for my own intolerance and unrepentance. I wrote her a letter of thanksgiving and repentance that day. I asked her and the Lord to forgive me for closing my heart and not following God's commandment. I'd learn there is joy in both forgiving and being forgiven. And I asked myself why I hadn't put the problem in the Lord's hands instead of hurting all those years.

That day God transformed her gift of flowers and

note into a lesson of forgiveness and a blessing for both of us. Grudges and anger are unacceptable to the Lord. Remember the words of Colossians 3:13, *Bear with each other and forgive whatever grievances you may have against one another Forgive as the Lord forgave you.*

Lord, you have told us over and over to forgive as we have been forgiven by you. Help us to let our frustration and anger step back so that we can forgive those who have hurt us in some way. Let us remember that You forgive us daily for our sins. In Jesus name, Amen.

From the Lips of Children

by Gail Gaymer Martin

Holiday family dinners arouse wonderful memories, and I treasure one such dinner a few years ago. The table overflowed with all the traditional mouth-watering delicacies. The family crowded around the table, strapping little ones into highchairs. This year Amanda was old enough to sit on a regular chair piled high with telephone books, and she posed liked a little lady as the adults gathered around the table.

Before the entire family was seated, one eager diner reached across Amanda's plate toward the turkey platter. She watched as the meat-filled fork swept past her again and was deposited on a dinner plate. Another adult grabbed a dinner roll and covered it with butter.

In silence, Amanda observed the activity. Then in a gentle, lilting voice, like a mother who tenderly reminds her child to be carefully, she said, "Fold your hands."

The adults turned to her as she sat with her head bowed and her tiny hands folded. Meekly the over-eager adults placed their forks down on their plates and folded their hands and bowed their heads for the table prayer.

I thought of the Child Jesus in the temple speaking to the learned men. We can learn a lesson from children. God's methods of guidance are awesome. In Matthew

21:16 (NIV) we read: *From the lips of children and infants you have ordained praise?*

Heavenly Father, Help us to live our lives and faith through the eyes of a child—with purity, trust, and faith. In Jesus name, Amen

In God's Time

by Gail Gaymer Martin

Every child is filled with dreams and "wannabes:" nurse, fireman, veterinarian, or some other careers. I wanted to be a writer, particularly a novelist. As early as third grade, I wrote poetry and received accolades from my teachers. Later I created my own series of Nancy Drew-type novels. In high school, I penned long romances and spent summers lying under our oak tree reading books I lugged home from the public library.

But my dream remained a dream. After college, I became an English teacher and forced high school students to read novels, hoping they would love books like I did.

But what about my writing? I wrote professional articles, newsletter material, humorous skits for church and teacher programs, and worship materials. But I wasn't the "real" published writer of my dreams.

After a master's degree and thirty-two years of teaching and working as a guidance counselor, I retired—or thought I did. Then, I learned that dreams are filled in God's time and not mine. Today God has blessed me with hundreds of published short stories and articles, numerous worship resource books, and, to my great joy, over 80 published novels.

Never give up a dream. Be patient and wait for the

Lord's bidding. When God deems us ready, matured and ripened, eager witnesses brimming with the Good News, in His good time, our treasured dreams can become a precious reality. *Be still before the Lord and wait patiently for him.* Psalms 37:7 (NIV)

Lord, we know that you answer our prayers in your time and not hours. Give us an open mind to know that you have heard our prayers and your answer will come when it is time. In Jesus name, Amen

Multi-award-winning novelist, Gail Gaymer Martin, is the author of Christian romance, romantic suspense, and women's fiction with more than 70 published novels and over four million books in print. Named one of the best novelists in the Detroit area by CBS local news, she is a founder of American Christian Fiction Writers, a member of Christian Author Network and Romance Writers of America. Gail is a keynote speaker and workshop presenter at conferences and women's events across the U.S. Find her novels on Amazon or www.gailgaymermartin.com

under Books/Novels. Contact Gail via her website or at P.O.Box 20054, Sedona, AZ 86341

Black Moment

By Darlene Franklin

*And that's when…the produce of the country will
give Israel's survivors something to be proud of again.
Oh, they'll hold their heads high!*
Isaiah 4:2 MSG

Fiction thrives on the black moment: when Darth Vader has killed Obi-Wan; when Gandalf falls at Mount Moria.

The first verse of Isaiah 4 is the blackest of black moments. Towards the end of the deportation of Israel into exile, only the dregs of society, "discards and rejects," were left behind. Their women felt so worthless, they ganged up, seven women to one man. *"We'll take care of ourselves, get our own food and clothes. Just give us a child. Make us pregnant so we'll have something to live for!"* (ISAIAH 4:1 MSG)

When the situation gets that desperate, that's when God steps in. His Branch will sprout green and lush. "God's Branch" is a picture of the Messiah. But for the people of Isaiah's day, it also spoke to an immediate need.

There would be food. Plenty of food. *Good* crops. "Something to be proud of again." The people would lift their heads high, and walk with a spring in their step.

And once God took care of their physical needs, He addressed their emotional needs. Every survivor was *precious*. Women wouldn't need to sell themselves, seven to one man.

God capped it off by addressing their spiritual needs: He "reclassified" them as holy and cleansed the people and the place of its immorality.

Restoration! Once again, healthy, confident, in right relationship with God. The story has come to a triumphant conclusion, Isaiah might have been tempted to end the book right there. Of course, God still had a lot more to say to and through him.

Contemporary women can identify with those-husband seeking women. In 2013, there were eighty-seven unmarried men for every one hundred unattached women.[1] As in ancient times, they hunger for a deeper life, with husband, children, fruit of one kind or another. Oh, how the promise of God's green branch still echoes in hearts.

Perhaps, Christians focus on the spiritual exchange. He added Christ's righteousness to their account, which cancelled out their sin debt. They don't quite understand and can never forget that gift.

But God knows that they are human, and He also makes them new in other ways. He provides for their physical needs and restores an appropriate sense of self, of worth and preciousness in His eyes.

God doesn't intend for Christians to live hang-dog lives, dejected and shame-faced. Instead, He promises to make them proud, so they will lift their heads high. Romans 12:3 is often quoted as a warning against pride: "Do not think of yourself more highly than you ought, but rather think of yourself with sober judgment."

---

[1] https://www.census.gov/newsroom/facts-for-features/2014/cb14-ff21.html

Behind the warning against puffing yourself up do you hear the echo—or more lowly than you ought. Abject self-abasement displeases God as much as pride. He created each person, unique, beautiful—perfect. When a person honestly assesses their uniqueness, pride and destructive humility falls by the wayside.

And that's just the beginning of their new story, one that will continue throughout eternity.

<u>Prayer</u>: Sovereign God, how I thank you that every black moment has a new beginning. You never close the door on us, never refuse to honor a repentant prayer. May people see the difference between in the before and after picture of Your transformation. Amen.

Credit Counselors

By Darlene Franklin

"Come now, let us settle the matter," says the Lord. "Though your sins are like scarlet, they shall be as white as snow. Though they are red as crimson, they shall be like wool."
ISAIAH 1:18 NIV

D ebt dogs the steps of many Americans today. Average credit debt is $16,140, impossible for most to pay off easily. And although bankruptcies have fallen annually since 2006, the latest figures indicate 800,000 individuals filed for bankruptcy in one year.

The higher the debt mounts, the less the credit card holder is able to pay on the principle, and the more creditors hound the debtor. They offer to "settle" the debt for a one-time payment far less than the full amount due.

Yet, even that offer is beyond the capacity of many to repay. One constant remains: they owe the debt, they have to pay or face the consequences—garnishment. Ruined credit. Bankruptcy.

The first verses of Isaiah read like a demand letter from God. *"Woe to the sinful nation, a people whose guilt is great!"* (Isaiah 1:4) Their list of sins grew longer and longer: rebellion, doing evil, corruption, forsaking the Lord, rotten fruit. God rejected the payment arrangements they offered—observance of the New Moon feasts and appointed festivals. He didn't listen to their many prayers.

God had already garnered their checks, so to speak, seeking payment for their sins. Their cities were laid desolate, ravaged by fire. Foreign raiders stripped their crops. Strangers laid waste to their fields. They continued charging more sin-debt to their account, and they had nothing to offer in repayment.

What ran through their minds when God offered to "settle the matter?" What more could God demand of them than they had already paid? What would God demand in exchange for their sinful debt?

Even when a creditor offers to settle a debt in good faith, those unable to pay will continue to avoid those kindly meant phone calls. They're no more able to repay $500 than $5,000.

Accountants describe assets in terms of black and red. Retailers count on the post-Thanksgiving, "Black Friday" shopping frenzy to put their business in the profit-making category. Otherwise, they may remain "in the red," loss instead of profit.

God paints sin with a fiery brush. also used red to demonstrate their debt. Their sins were like scarlet, red like crimson. But his offer didn't slash the debt or lighten it to pink. He offered to wipe it out, clean it away, returning their status to a zero balance, pure white.

The Israelites had two choices. If they accepted God's offer of a zero balance, and became willing and obedient, they would enjoy the good things of the land.

But if they refused, an even worse fate awaited them. They would die by the sword.

In the New Testament, Jesus wiped out the sin debt by covering it in a sea of red—His blood. People have two choices: believe and receive eternal life (John 3:16)—or suffer condemnation for their unbelief.

Prayer: Almighty God, when You call me to account for my sins, I can offer no excuses, make no payments. By grace You paid the debt for me. But You didn't spend heavenly dollars. Not even Jesus' perfect life settled the bill. It took every drop of His lifeblood to cancel my debt. Amazing grace! How sweet the sound! When I've been in heaven for ten thousand years, I will barely have begun to praise You. Now, today, may my life show that new beginning. Wash me and I shall be whiter than snow. In Jesus's name, amen.

Walking With God

Come, let us go up to the mountain of the LORD, to the temple of the God of Jacob. He will teach us his ways, so that we may walk in his paths.
ISAIAH 2:3 NIV

By Darlene Franklin

Every four years people from across the globe stream to mountains in a single place on earth. The Olympic torch moves from one city to another until athletes gather to battle in peace.

One day people will gather at the mountain of the Lord, not for a short two weeks, but forever. The illusion of cooperation at the Olympics will be replaced by the reality of God's peace as He judges the nations. "Ain't going to study war no more—" the words of the African American spiritual echoes the words of verse four of Isaiah 2.

Oh, how the verses call to a deep longing for peace.

The coming of the Prince of Peace to create the peaceable kingdom is a future promise. It won't happen until the last days, according to Isaiah.

But the instructions for living in and preparing for that kingdom started in Isaiah's day and will continue until kingdom come. Even now, believers need to prepare.

Get to a place where they can learn God's ways. (verse 3) Although the body of Christ gathers for study and worship, they don't have to move to a pre-selected location to be a church. The Spirit of God lives within them and guides them into all truth. As they learn they will:

Walk in God's paths (verse 3). The Spirit not only teaches believers, He also turns their hearts to obedience, And as they walk in God's paths and learn His ways, they will...

Exchange their weapons for tools. Swords for plowshares, pruning hooks for spears. The plowshare retains the sharp point of the sword, as the pruning hook does for spears. God turns their weapons of war, their personalities, their skills, from destruction to peace.

Isaiah gets so excited about the future that he calls to the descendants of Jacob to "walk

in the light of the Lord." In the words of the later hymnist, "When we walk with the Lord in the light of His word, what a glory He sheds on our way."

God will establish His kingdom, but He calls for the active participation of His people. He doesn't say, "come and be blessed." He doesn't threaten to destroy their weapons. Instead, He invites them to transformation. They are to see and walk and change.

The road to God's mountain is magnetic. Your small throng will swell as all nations, the unexpected, the unchurched, the anti-Christian and atheist, join the stream to God's kingdom.

That's the power God is offering. In the end, everyone will see and acknowledge Him as Lord. Today, believers can move, change, walk—and catch glimpses of that beautiful future as through a glass darkly.

Prayer: God of the mountain, I want to join You on that mountaintop. But it won't happen for me

quite as easily as it did for Peter, James and John at Jesus' transfiguration (Mark 9:2). I have to get moving. The more I know of Your Word, the more I absorb it into the roots of my being, the more it ekes into my every action and thought. The farther I walk, the more I walk in Your light. Lead me, change, transform me into an instrument of peace and a beacon to lead others to Your mountain. Amen.

All's Well

By Darlene Franklin

Tell the righteous it will be well with them, for they will enjoy the fruit of their deeds.
Isaiah 3:10, NIV

The mountaintop experience in chapter two has vanished. Judah's lifelines have been cut off. They have become a stench in God's nostrils.

In a passage like this, readers are apt to rush through the account of doom and gloom. Don't skip ahead too fast. Tucked into the warnings of thundering judgment, God inserts the fate of the righteous. A single verse, eighteen short words, broadcasts the good news: God won't reject the righteous with the ungodly.

Who are the righteous? Those have been made right with God through Christ the Lord. As Paul says, "How much more will those who receive God's abundant provision of grace and of the gift of righteousness reign in life through the one man, Jesus Christ!" (Romans 5:17 NIV)

God's two-fold promise throws a lifeline of hope to the righteous. The first promise is *It will be well with them.*

God promises, not protection *from* disaster, but *through* it. Horatio Spofford wrote the beloved hymn "It is well with my soul" after he learned his daughters had died in a shipwreck. His wife informed him, "I survived alone."

Spofford insisted, "It is well with my soul" both in times of peace and when buffeted by sea billows. He trusted the unchanging God.

When David was fleeing from King Saul, he said, "The Lord has rewarded me according to my righteousness" (Psalm 18:20 NIV). How could David say that after Saul had tried to kill him?

He reassures believers that God will respond according to the measure of their faith. "To the faithful You show yourself faithful, to the blameless You show yourself blameless, to the pure You show yourself pure." (Psalm 18:25-26 NIV)

Isaiah;s second promise adds to the first: *they will enjoy the fruit of their deeds.*

How the original readers must have rejoiced in that promise. They lived among people stripped of supply and support (verse 1). Oppression was the rule of the day (verse five). The situation was so bad, no one wanted a position of leadership. Their women didn't have the use of all the stuff they use to make themselves beautiful.

But the righteous would enjoy the fruit of their deeds. They would continue to bear fruit, given by God, and no one would snatch it from their hands.

God's promise holds out hope today. His children are not of this world, although they are in this world. When they experience heartache and disaster, it will be well with them. The faithful God remains with them. Like David, like Spofford, let them choose to say, "It is well with my soul."

In a world without meaning, God offers purpose. His people will enjoy the fruit of their hands, although not necessarily in wealth or success as the world defines it.

Let tribulation come. Let the sea billows roll. It will be well for the righteous, and they will continue to enjoy the fruit of their hands.

Prayer: **Lord Almighty, how thankful I am that You don't treat the righteous and the wicked equally. You send the rain on the just and the unjust, and every living thing is affected the fallen world. But You never leave the righteous alone with unrelenting discouragement. Oh, Lord, how I praise You that it will be well with me. That I will enjoy fruit bearing. That You aren't done with me! Amen.**

Best-selling hybrid author Darlene Franklin's greatest claim to fame is that she writes full-time from a nursing home. *Mermaid Song* is her fiftieth unique title! She's also contributed to more than twenty nonfiction titles. Her column, "The View Through my Door," appears in five monthly venues. Her most recent titles are *Seven Brides for Seven Mail-Order Husbands* and *Acadian Hearts*. You can find her online at: Website and blog, Facebook, Amazon author page

Darlene Franklin

Writing at the Crossroads of Love and Grace

Latest releases: *To Riches Again* and *Pony Express Romance Collection*

http://darlenefranklinwrites.com/

Turn Your Eyes

By Martha Rogers

"Whether you turn to the right or left, your ears will hear a voice behind you, saying, 'This is the way; walk in it.'"
Isaiah 30:21

Distractions of everyday life and things happening around us may cause us to turn away from our focus on what we are doing. Our enemy causes major distractions because the enemy is in opposition to us and what we are doing.

Usually the smaller distractions of our children or home only take us away from our tasks for short periods and are necessary to keep our families running smoothly. The larger distractions in life come in many forms from a major illness to a financial setback.

The Lord wants us to have success. He cheers us on to victory. We hear His voice behind us telling us the way to go, but the enemy is always lurking around the corner to see how he can cause trouble and disharmony in our lives. He can take good things and turn them to his ways just as God can take the bad things and turn them to good. Remember, too, that the enemy is persistent.

We must be ever vigilant against the wiles of our enemy. He comes in many forms, even through our families and friends. We must focus on what God is telling us and where God is leading us, not what others have to say.

Satan can attack and distract us with a few unkind words, a rejection from a boss or leader, negative remarks from a friend or family member. He loves to plant seeds of doubt, pull us away from our focus and cause us to lose sight of God's plan.

The song "Turn Your Eyes Upon Jesus" tells us to "look full in his wonderful face."

When we do, the distractions fade away and we are able to bask in the light of His glory and grace. Let us listen to that voice from behind telling us, "this is the way; walk in it."

Heavenly Father, may our sight be focused on You to day. May our eyes be fully trained on You so that we hear Your voice telling us the way we should go.

Martha Rogers is a freelance author of both fiction and non-fiction and a speaker. Her stories and articles have appeared in a number of compilations and magazines. Her first fiction novella released in 2007.

Her experiences as a public school teacher, Sunday school teacher, youth leader, First Place leader, Mom and Grandmother give Martha a unique field of ministry.

Martha is am alumni of CLASS and is available to speak at Women's Retreats, conferences, and luncheons on topics of interest to women of all ages.

As an author, she is available to speak at writing conferences and workshops on a variety of topics of interest to writers.

Social Media:
Facebook: Martha L. Rogers
Twitter: @MarthaRogers2
Website: www.marthawrogers.com

Pinterest: www.pinterest.com/grammymartha/

The Peace That Passes Understanding

In Honor of my Parents
By Kimberly Grist

As a child, I remember many occasions where Psalm 127:3-5 was quoted to my father.

Behold, children are a gift of the LORD, The fruit of the womb is a reward. Like arrows in the hand of a warrior, so are the children of one's youth. How blessed is the man whose quiver is full of them; They will not be ashamed. When they speak with their enemies in the gate. (Psalm 127:3-5, NASB)

Inevitably the scripture always brought out a chuckle. As a child, I didn't understand that the reference was to a bag that contains arrows. Being one of seven children, I just assumed it had to do with a house full of kids with one working bathroom. I can testify that our home was most definitely "full." Although my family's "quiver" is not quite as full as my parents', I certainly understand one message of these verses, is to count my children as blessings.

What is a quiver anyway? Simply put, it is a bag or a container that holds arrows. God is creating a picture in our mind of a warrior ready with his bow and a bag full of arrows. So, at the risk of creating a bad pun, the point here is to aim, take deliberate action toward the goal of loving God.

We as parents are to be intentional about training our children in the way of the Lord.

As a child, my church attendance was marginal. Religious instruction was in the form of Bible stories and song. My Mother liked to sing but she always messed up the words. As a child, I had no idea the words weren't correct and would sing them with all my heart.

The phrase if Mama wasn't happy nobody is happy was the understatement of the century in my family. We all learned quickly to do as we were told. So, if she said sing, we sang. I remember one of her favorites was; I have the Joy, Joy, Joy, Joy down in my heart. One of the verses was I have the peace that passes understanding down in my heart. But we didn't sing it that way but sang "I have a peaceapasa understanding down in my heart."

I recall asking my Mom for a definition of a peaceapasa. She answered that she didn't know but to sing it anyway…and so we did.

Much later as an adult reading the bible verse From Philippians 4:6-8. I called my brother and said, "I know what a peaceapasa is.

Philippians 4:6-8 6 Be careful for nothing; but in everything by prayer and supplication with thanksgiving let your requests be made known unto God.7 And the peace of God, which passeth all understanding, shall keep your hearts and minds through Christ Jesus. 8 Finally, brethren, whatsoever things are true, whatsoever things are honest, whatsoever things are just, whatsoever things are pure, whatsoever things are lovely, whatsoever things are of good report; if there be any virtue, and if there be any praise, think on these things.

Now I know that a peaceapassa is the best thing ever. We can have the peace of God that passes all understanding in Christ Jesus.

You may think this sounds crazy, and that's okay. But there is a God who loves us so much that He sent His only Son who lived a perfect life to come and die on a cross for all of our sins.

And not only has he paid the penalty for our sins so that those who admit our sins and accept his gift will live forever in heaven....

He wants to be an active part of our life. He wants us to cast all our troubles on him.

This is how we know what love is. *Jesus Christ laid down His life for us...*1 John 3:16. (NIV)

Father God,
Thank You for Your Word and the beautiful picture of love and redemption it paints throughout. Enable us to be like the warrior, let our lives be the arrows that point to The Way, The Truth and The Light. Thank You that You loved us so much so that You came in person, God incarnate, to show us how to live and gave Your life as the perfect sacrifice for our sins. How grateful we are that even when we fail, Your love and compassion does not.

May you all receive the peace of understanding through Christ Jesus.
Blessings,
Kimberly Grist

Kim Grist is married to her high school sweetheart, Pastor Nelson Grist, who serves as Pastor of First Baptist Church Orchard Hill in Griffin, Georgia. She likes to refer to herself as a mother of three special sons, one with special needs. Kim is pictured to the left with two of those special sons, Zachary in the center and Micah behind. Her other son is Christopher (not pictured).

Kim is also a grandmother and proud to be a child of the living God. She feels called to help and encourage others and to share experiences both good and bad in order to be the witness that God would have us to be.

Because she and her husband have an adult son with Down syndrome, she has a passion to encourage others in offering a special needs ministry in the church. She finds that many times it's not just the handicapped child or adult that doesn't attend church but the disability of one segregates the whole family from church attendance.

Because she did not grow up in church she believes that her perspective on what Sunday School is or could or should be is sometimes different from other people. She strives to find ways to make Sunday School and Children's Church an experience that helps nurture a love for Christ and to help them to grow in a true relationship with Him, even if it means going back to the drawing board. When preparing for a lesson she finds that she often wants to add or change something in the lesson to make it better. "The unfortunate side of being creative in this respect is not always positive", Kim says. "Often my attempts fail and I end up looking like an old episode, of I Love Lucy." "But on the occasion that something really connects, it is important to share it. After all, isn't that what being part of the body of Christ is all about?

Take a look at Kim's blog on Sunday School Zone   @ https://sundayschoolzone.com/category/the-sunday-school-zone-blog/kim-grist/

And for more ideas on a Special Needs Ministry @

https://christianindex.org/kim-grist-special-needs-child/

https://christianindex.org/the-continuing-saga-of-kim-grist-and-her-special-needs-son/kim-and-zach-grist-slider/

Connect with Kimberly:

Facebook https://www.facebook.com/FaithFunandFriends/

Twitter https://twitter.com/GristKimberly

Amazon Author Page https:/www.amazon.com/Kimberly-Grist/e/B07H2NTJ71

Website https://kimberlygrist.com

A Timeless Message in a Bottle

By Stacey Hitch

Jesus spent a lot of time around water; I like to think He liked the beach. When I go to the beach I look at all the elements that make up the ocean. I can see God's wonderful lessons and blessings expressed in the waves, a jetty, and even the sand. Sometimes I stand upon the shore pondering the vastness and the depth of God's Love for me. Ocean waves are truly astounding, each time a wave crashes onto the shore it carries away some sand from one place to another. The waves, sand, and beach will always change.

God deals with our sin in the same way.

His waves of mercy and grace wash over us and take away our sins. God also wants us to be like a jetty. A jetty is an armored structure mostly made up of huge rocks that extends out into the water and is intended to protect a navigation channel. He wants us to put on our full armor, to stand firm, but allow His Word to penetrate every nook and cranny to get past the rocks, enabling His complete unconditional love into our hearts.

My message for you: Jesus loves you! God sent His only Son, Jesus, to rescue you, to show you how to love Him, to teach you and to bring you home! I have found in my journey the hardest thing to do is to love myself. Too many times we cry out and repent of our sins to the Lord, then we go back and reflect on our sins over and over.

The reality is that if you've asked God to forgive you and asked Jesus to come into your life — you are forgiven!!! His Word says so. "If we confess our sins, He is faithful and just to forgive us our sins, and to cleanse us from all unrighteousness" (1 John 1:9 KJV). God wants us to realize that His love and forgiveness includes His forgetfulness.

The enemy delights in holding up our past sins and trying to get us to agree with him that we are disappointments. If, of course, we are having a bad day and all heck is breaking loose in our lives, we easily believe the enemy's lies.

If you repeatedly allow the enemy to bring your past sins into the present, they will be used to beat you down until you give up and go back to your sinful ways. How can you crush the enemy when he brings up your past? Send the enemy to Jesus, there is so much power in the name of Jesus! Let Jesus do the work for you!

As hard as it is at times, remember that Jesus loves you. And you can love yourself no matter what your sins were. The Word of God tells us in Matthew 19:19 (KJV) "You shall love your neighbor as yourself." Sometimes the most difficult person to love, forgive, or even accept is the one who appears before you in the mirror.

Jesus is telling you that proper self-love is acceptable. One thing I have learned is you will never truly love others as long as you're at battle within your heart. Jesus is simply telling you that you are to love yourself the way God loves you, in His image, purpose, and of course for His Glory.

To love yourself as God loves you, you need to dig deeper. You must seek after His best for you. You need to conform yourself to God's expectations, live according to His guidelines and precepts in the Bible. He has so much love for you and He gave you a compass just like the ships have at sea, but our compass is the Bible. We must learn to yield our desires and allow His will to be done. You will find peace with an abundance of joy, love, and the ability to live a functional and fruitful life.

Your past does not have to poison your future so let it go! Jesus loves you and sees a treasure in you. Rejoice in your relationship with Him. Don't quit; dig deeper and mature in new heights with Jesus. Together we must finish this race to victory!

We are nearing the end of the race. Christ is coming soon to bring us to our home with Him. Until then, if enough of us send out ripples of love, those ripples can turn into waves of love to reach the lost souls of this world. It may seem like an overwhelming undertaking, but with the power of Jesus we can do it! People, we need God more than ever. Don't run from God. Run to Him. He loves you!

"Wherefore seeing we also are compassed about with so great a cloud of witnesses, let us lay aside every weight, and the sin which doth so easily beset us, and let us run with patience the race that is set before us, looking unto Jesus the author and finisher of our faith; who for the joy that was set before Him endured the cross, despising the shame, and is set down at the right hand of the throne of God" (Hebrews 12:1-2 KJV).

Jesus' message in a bottle for you: I love you, you are My treasure. Don't quit!

Trinity Social Media Marketing is a full-service social media marketing agency located on the Eastern Shore. We all know Social Media is in it for the long haul and it can be confusing, frustrating, or just plain tedious when you are a busy business owner. That's where Trinity Social Media Marketing comes in. We work with you to create a social media strategy that is tailor-made just for your brand and your goals. We build our campaigns around what's most important to you, whether it be promoting your products, explaining your services, or gaining fans. Whatever your goals are, we'll work with you to achieve them. #socialmedia Facebook Management, Twitter Management, Instagram Management, Pinterest Management, Blog, Content, Training/Consultant.

https://www.facebook.com/hitch1725

Trinity Media Marketing

A Shelter in the Storm

By Leann Harris

Psalm 16:1-2 *Keep me safe, my God, For in you I take refuge.*

There are days when it feels like you're up against the wall from the time you wake. When that happens these words are for you. You can count on the Lord to be with you. He is there for you no matter what you feel. It's a promise. God keeps his promises. If you believe and trust, those feeling of doubt will disappear.

Lord, let me take this scripture to heart, and when doubts assail me, let me claim my refuge in you. I'll not rely on how I feel, but choose you.

Leann Harris was born at Fitzsimmons Army Hospital there in Denver and grew up in the city until her family moved to Houston. Rural Colorado & ranches are two of her favorite topics.

More books by Leann Harris

STAR-SPANGLED HOMECOMING

LAST TRUTH

LAST LIE

STOLEN SECRETS

Storms

By Helen Gray

Two blasts from a thunderstorm fried our TV, modem, router, land line, kitchen stove, and hot water heater. Then the bathroom stool had to be fixed, followed by the washer quitting and having to be replaced. Later, I parked my car at church and couldn't get out of it. The door latch had to be replaced. Then I went to open the storm door—and the handle fell off. I felt I was under siege.

For the past two years my husband (80 his next birthday) has been ailing. He's on medications for multiple issues—heart, diabetes, blood pressure, etc.—and is exhibiting delated symptoms from a light stroke suffered a few years ago from which we thought he had fully recovered. So a good deal of our time is spent driving to doctor appointments and waiting for test results—the current one a brain MRI.

What to do when the well runs dry?

First, I have to remind myself that God doesn't promise we won't have bad things won't happen to us, or that we won't have to endure trials and problems. Then I remember how Job suffered, het he said, "When He has tested me, I shall come forth as gold." (Job 23:10)

Only God knows what paths we will have to travel, but we have His assurance that, "I am with you always."

(Matthew 28:2) And that "All things work together for good to those who love God." (Romans 8:28) May we each remember that, no matter how difficult our storms may be, or how hopeless our future may look, God's presence can provide us with the courage and strength we need, and that we won't be alone.

Though our trials send us to our knees, and our tears flow like rivers, day by day let's trust His promises and find strength to meet our trials and give us each day what He deems best. He's always near us and knows our cares and needs. As we travel life's road, let's trust God to lift our heavy loads. For He also said, "Come to me, all you who labor and are heavy laden, and I will give you rest." (Matthew 11:28)

The storms that threaten to destroy us, God will use to strengthen us.

http://www.helenbrowngray.com

Helen Gray grew up in a small Missouri town and married her pastor. While working alongside her husband in his ministry, she had three children, taught school, directed/accompanied church music programs, and became an amateur ventriloquist. Now retired, with the three children gone from the nest, she and her supportive husband still live in their native Missouri Ozarks where he roams the woods, hunts and fishes, and she weaves stories meant to honor God and depict Christian lives and problems as she knows and observes them. Helen thanks God for the time and opportunity to write and considers it an added blessing if her stories touch others in even a small way.

Take a Seat

and Watch
God's Goodness Pass By.

By Betty Slade

A question was presented to the Writers of Faith. "Why would the readers of the Matter of Faith Column want your faith? How does your readers identify with your voice of faith?

Moses asked God to show him His glory, God show him his goodness.

The Lord said to Moses, *"I will make all My goodness pass before you, and I will proclaim the name of the Lord before you."* Exodus 33:19

As I pondered this thought, the Spirit of Christ swept over me as if to say, "You cannot understand My glory without personally experiencing My goodness."

The Spirit continued to speak to me. "I was there when you wanted to throw away your marriage. You could have lost your children. I saved you from yourself. I listened to your prayers, when you begged Me for things that would have destroyed you. I wouldn't give them to you and you were angry with Me."

"I could have stopped you at any time, but I didn't. I

knew the worst in you. You didn't know what was in your heart, but I did and I knew what you were capable of doing, both good and bad. You had to see it for yourself. My grace covered you and the lessons were better for you than the sin and pain you suffered."

"I was there when you sat in the hospital room with your son. His leg was broken in hundreds of pieces. I even allowed the doctors to doubt their ability to save his leg. I pulled the veil back on the spirit world that night and you saw my angels diligently working on his crooked leg. They made it straight. I made you aware that I was there with you. Your son walks with a slight limp today as a reminder of how I valued his wholeness and saved him from greater pain."

"I was there every time your son overdosed, and I spared his life and spared you the heartache of burying a teenage child."

"I was in the car with you on Cumbres Pass, when you slid off the icy road where the mountain drops down a mile. I put that barbwire fence there to catch you thirty feet on your way down. You climbed that steep incline praising My name. I chuckled at your enthusiasm, as you spoke to the man who stopped to help you. He looked, shook his head in disbelief and asked. "How did you survive?" It was My goodness, which passed by.

"I gave you a sense of humor and laughter to help you deal with life, which has not been neat and tidy. You had things in your heart that needed to be dealt with. I forgave you. I knew one day you would learn about my love.

"I gave you a thirst for learning and yet you were deprived of college and a higher education. It has made you hungry for knowledge. I gave you a hard beginning so you would fight for understanding and a better station in life."

"I pulled you out of dark dreary places, where you insisted on walking and where my angels feared to tread. I was there and led you through the darkness."

So, as I, a Writer of Faith, lay my soul bare, I ask myself the question, why do I believe? Why would readers want my faith?

I believe it is because I've seen the goodness of God pass by me. I have known His presence in the worst of times and the best of times. I have been captured by His love. He hid me in the cliff of the Rock and showed me not only the tragic things, which He spared me from, but He has shown me his goodness. I **have** seen His Glory.

The Lord said to Moses, "I will proclaim the name of the Lord before you." He has done that for me. His Holy Spirit has passed by me through His Son, Jesus. His life bought and paid for my entrance into a world of love and goodness. That is why I witness and proclaim my faith.

When God told Moses to sit over there and hide in the cleft, He showed him His goodness? Did Moses see the depth of his own wretchedness in order to see clearly God's goodness? I don't know, but for me, it seems to be that way.

Betty J. Slade is an author of fiction and non-fiction, a newspaper columnist, and an artist in oils and watercolors. She painted the cover and character portraits in her book *Spirit of the Red Candle, Journal of Mary Magdalene* (Blanco Dove, March 2013). In 2017, Forget Me Not Romances, a division of Winged Publications published *Heart Bender* Book 1—Sangre de Cristo Mountains, a four-book series. *Under Heaven's Rage*, a story of a Colorado rancher's wife, is ready for a publisher.

She writes a weekly column for the Pagosa *SUN, The Artist Lane,* about small town living, and especially about her husband, Sweet Al, in Pagosa Springs, Colorado. *Living on the Front Page* (Blanco Dove, January 2013) is a published collection of her selected Artist Lane articles from 2008-2012. She and a team of 18 current Faith Writers are contributors to *A Matter of Faith, a* weekly column for the *SUN.*

Betty published two Bible study books, *The King's Choice*, based on the Old Testament book *Song of Solomon* (Blanco Dove, March 2013) and *Cameo, A Study of Ruth,* and a thumbnail sketch of the history of Israel and its redeemer. (Blanco Dove, second edition, March 2013) She self-published two books of poetry and painted the book covers for all her books until 2016.

Her art is displayed on the Princess Cruise Line, and in her Pagosa Springs' private gallery and studio in the Rocky Mountains of Colorado. She is the Vice President of Wolf Creek Writers Network. She and Al live in Pagosa Springs, Colorado. They have four children and four grandchildren.

Learn more about Betty and view additional social media contacts at http://www.bettyjslade.com/ She enjoys hearing from readers at betty@bettyslade.com.

Dreams Change

By Cynthia Hickey

I've been making up stories since I was little. Almost since the time I learned to read. Interestingly enough, I wanted to be a teacher. Being an author didn't occur to me in any shape or form, although I always wrote my stories down. No, I was pretty emphatic about being a teacher.

Funny how God often has other plans. I didn't go to college (kind of need to in order to be a teacher). I got married right out of high school when my boyfriend joined the Air Force. It wasn't until my second marriage and almost twenty years later that I became a teacher of sorts. First, girl scouts, then Sunday school for ten years, then foster care for nine more years, then I worked in an Elementary School as a Detention Monitor, and now I teach workshops on writing. Maybe not a teacher in the normal sense, but still a teacher all the same.

And, I keep writing my stories down. While working at the Elementary School, I had opportunities to write while supervising students. As time went by, I wrote more and dealt less with children. My dream changing.

Or…was teaching ever what I was meant to do in the first place? Perhaps teaching truly was only a child's dream. The trials of my life have led me to this point. Had even one thing changed, I might not be making a living doing what I love…a job that enables me to hang at conferences with like-minded peeps, stay at home with hair undone and no makeup, wearing comfy clothes. I can set my own hours, even write while traveling.

Yes, I'm convinced I'm right where I was meant to be.

Jeremiah 29:11 – For I know the plans I have for you," declares the LORD, "plans to prosper you and not to harm you, plans to give you hope and a future.

Lord, may I always take the time to ask what your plans for my life are. Hold me steady until the time is right.

Website at www.cynthiahickey.com

Multi-published and Amazon and ECPA Best-Selling author Cynthia Hickey has sold over a million copies of her works since 2013. She has taught a Continuing Education class at the 2015 American Christian Fiction Writers conference, several small ACFW chapters and RWA chapters. She and her husband run the small press, Winged Publications, which includes some of the CBA's best well-known authors. She lives in Arizona with her husband, one of their seven children, two dogs, one cat, and three box turtles. She has nine grandchildren who keep her busy and tell everyone they know that "Nana is a writer".

Connect with me on FaceBook
Twitter
Bookbub
Sign up for my newsletter and receive a free short story
www.cynthiahickey.com

Follow me on Amazon
Bookbub

Caring for Aging Parents

By Debby Mayne

"I consider that our present sufferings are not worth comparing with the glory that will be revealed in us."
~Romans 8:18 NIV

As your parents age, you may feel that they (or you) are alone in the suffering that comes when our humanly bodies fail us. Remember that Paul went through years of the type of horrendous suffering that very few people will ever experience in today's world. While it's not easy to focus outside of the pain you and your parents are dealing with at the present time, Christ calls on us to trust Him and to remember the eternal promises of God.

It's much easier to wallow in the pain and suffering we have to endure on earth than to focus on what we have to look forward to when Christ calls us home. During the aging process may see your parents become crippled, feeble, or confused, but deep down, they are still the people who sacrificed for you, raised you, and helped you to become the person you are today. Rather than view them as burdens, take a step back and see the blessings in their provisions for you through the years.

When Christ returns, God's glory will be revealed as his promises come to fruition. The current pain you and your parents are dealing with will still be present until He calls us home, but the magnificence of being with Him will make it all worthwhile. ~ Debby Mayne

Prayer: Dear Lord, heavenly Father, thank you for the blessing of loving parents. Please give me the strength and ability to care for them as needed. I pray all of this in Jesus' name. Amen.

Please visit Debby Mayne at the following places: Website: Debbymayne.net Facebook: Debby Mayne, Author Twitter: @DebbyMayne

Debby Mayne is the author of more than 80 books and novellas in the romance, mystery, and Southern women's fiction genres. She and her husband live in North Carolina near their beautiful daughters, handsome sons-in-law, precious granddaughters, and an assortment of grand kitties and grand puppies.

Debby's Books

Christmas Romance: Christmas in Oak Creek John's Christmas Bride Christmas in Winter Creek Christmas in Colorado Carolina Christmas

Romance: Hollister Sisters Mail Order Brides (Historical) A Rose for Rose (Historical) Love Reigns (Contemporary) Love in the Low Country (Contemporary) Love's Image (Contemporary) Double Blessings (Contemporary) Against the Sunset (Contemporary) Bicycle Built for Two (contemporary) Love's Image (Contemporary) If the Dress Fits (Contemporary) Trouble in Paradise: Belles in the City Book 1 (Contemporary) One Foot Out the Door: Belles in the City Book 2 (Contemporary) Can't Fool Me Twice: Belles in the City Book 3 (Contemporary)

Mysteries: Murder Under the Mistletoe Gun in the Garden Offed at the Office

Investing in Our Children

By Cindy M. Amos

Over last weekend, my oldest son packed up and moved his possessions to an apartment as he starts his first full-time job half-way across the state of Kansas. His aerospace engineering degree coupled with a NASA internship researching rocket launches prepared the way for him to find promising work with rubber formulation at a large tire manufacturing plant.

When I woke him as a toddler to witness the night launches of the space shuttle from our driveway in south Florida, I would never have imagined the indelible setting of a course that would start him toward such success. For now, he makes large equipment tires. In the future, his aspirations are fixed on space exploration!

Standing at the door of his galaxy-decorated bedroom, I decide to leave it like this for now—a stable launch pad that fledged an engineer to a remarkable career under the guiding hand of God. The mess left behind is kind of endearing to a mom who remembers and holds fondly the journey from spectator to specialist.

Perhaps the term "entry level" applies more to the mother anyway, as I begin to navigate toward an empty nest. Praise God I still have my engineer-to-be youngest son in college, who—on rare occasions—professes to need the wisdom of his parents.

Lord, help us invest in our children selflessly, so that under your Almighty hand, they might learn to soar. Amen.

How great is the love the Father has lavished on us, that we should be called the children of God. 1 John 3:1

And that is what we are!

Cindy M. Amos lives and writes inspirational fiction from Wichita, Kansas. With her background in natural resources management and endangered species conservation, she typically writes about man living close to the land. "America's Fabulous Fifties" is her first historical regional romance sequel, allowing her to feature her transplanted homeland, the American Midwest, in its post-war pride. Married to an aviation engineer with two college-aged engineering sons, science rules the roost at the Amos home. On weekends, the author helps work on the family's fifth generation ranch in the Flint Hills of central Kansas near historic Council Grove. She enjoys nature, wildflowers, riding her bike along Rails to Trails, gardening, and home-canning. She can also throw a mean made-from-scratch cherry pie on the dinner table when the occasion suits her fancy. Her books are available on Amazon.

Member: American Christian Fiction Writers (South Central Kansas Chapter Secretary)

Review her full book-list on her website at:
http://cindymamos.wixsite.com/natureink

Also check her Amazon author page at:
https://www.amazon.com/Cindy-M.-Amos/e/B01JTDIPOQ/ref=dbs_p_ebk_rwt_abau

Find her on Facebook at:
https://www.facebook.com/natureinkbooks

Anniversary Blues

By Lisa Flickinger

H appy Anniversary," I said to myself looking at the mound of wet clothes in the dryer. After thirty years, I assumed Matt knew how to put the filter in properly. It appears he did not. The dryer door bounced against the filter and stayed open. Thus, my fat jeans were a sopping mess and I needed them to go out in public. Anyone who tells you working your way through party size bags of Cheetos, dill pickle chips, and pretzels will not make a crisis smoother is lying. They all made me feel better about Matt losing his job; however, not fitting into my regular jeans brought on my current situation.

Perhaps the man was a little distracted. He'd just lost a job he held for over thirty-three years and planned to retire in. Since then, odd events had begun occurring in the house like finding the cardboard recycling on the fridge shelf or discovering the garbage he'd taken out to the curb still in the garage.

He wasn't the only one. An hour later when I went to put the next load of laundry in the dryer I noticed fine blue speckles on the sheets, my bras, towels etc. I'd left a pen in a pocket (something I haven't done since year one). The pen broke during the wash cycle and the ink refill lodged in one of the holes (ink side out). As the laundry turned in the drum the tip of the refill dispersed its fine decoration throughout the entire load. Arggh!

Life is full of events which knock your world off centre and it's easy to slip into harassing one another about the small things, the things you can control. We have to force ourselves to remember the Lord asks us to encourage one another just as He encourages us.

"Blessed be the God and Father of our Lord Jesus Christ, the Father of mercies and God of all comfort, who comforts us in all our affliction, so that we may be able to comfort those who are in any affliction, with the comfort with which we ourselves are comforted by God." *(2 Cor. 1:3-4 ESV)*

I think Matt got it right. Later in the day I came home to find a beautiful anniversary gift waiting for me.

Dear Father,
Help me to be encouraging and understanding toward my husband just as You are with me.
In the name of Jesus, Amen

Wife of one, mother of three, and grandmother of nine. I live and write in the shadow of the Rocky Mountains. My journey to publication began in the stacks of our local library where I devoured fiction as a young girl and created small books out of construction paper.

When I'm not writing or reading, you will find me combing through antique shops, walking in the woods with my faithful Labrador Zeke, or sipping a Creme Brulee latte with friends.

The release of my first novel All That Glitters fulfills the lifelong dream of sharing the characters in my head with you, dear reader. Enjoy!

Follow me on Amazon

Choices

By Colleen L. Reece

"Take therefore no thought for the morrow: for the morrow shall take thought for the things of itself. Sufficient unto the day is the evil thereof" (Matthew 6:3, KJV).

Two prunes lay on a small boy's otherwise-empty plate.

"Eat your prunes," his mother said.

The boy shook his head. Eat those wrinkled things that stared up at him like a pair of watching eyes? Never!

"Eat your prunes," his mother repeated. When he stubbornly refused, she resorted to a last-ditch effort to get him to obey. "If you don't eat your prunes, you will make God awfully angry."

The threat didn't accomplish what she hoped. After long moments of silence, she gave up, sent her son to bed, and threw the prunes into the garbage.

Several hours later, a storm awakened her. Thunder bellowed. Rain beat the earth with a vengeance. Trees crashed. Jagged lightning pierced the darkness, making the world as bright as day.

Fearing that her son would be terrified, the woman slipped into a robe and ran to his room. A particularly bright flash of lightning showed an empty bed.

Fear swept over the mother. Where was her son?

A series of flashes disclosed a small, pajama-clad figure by the window. Hands on his hips, a teddy bear clutched under one arm, the child peered out at the wild night.

The mother's relief mingled with irritation. In a moment of silence between thunder booms, she opened her mouth to reprimand her son for being out of bed. Before she

could speak, she saw him shake his head. Then she heard him sigh and say in his childish, plaintive voice.

"Such a fuss to make over two prunes, God."

. . .

Hopefully, the mother never again resorted to threats about God becoming angry in order to control her son's behavior. Did an image of the little boy at the window etch itself indelibly into her heart and mind? The disappointment in his voice that Someone as big as the God he had been taught to love and respect would throw a tantrum over two, uneaten prunes? Let us hope so.

Sadly, there are persons who carry an equally distorted image of our Heavenly Father. Instead of focusing on God's love and forgiveness, they believe our inability to be perfect at all times brings down the wrath of God. This doctrine of fear is in direct opposition to the picture Jesus paints in Luke

4:18 (KJV).

"The Spirit of the Lord is upon me, because he hath anointed me to preach the gospel to the poor; he hath sent me to heal the brokenhearted, to preach deliverance to the captives, and recovering of sight to the blind, to set at liberty them that are bruised. . .
"

Life is filled with beauty, goodness, and joy, as well as disappointments, setbacks, worries great and small. Troubles may loom like skyscrapers or be of less significance than two prunes. It is all a matter of perspective.

Lord, thank You for helping me to banish fear and rely on You in both sunshine and storms. Amen.

Keys to Contentment

By Colleen L. Reece

"I have learned, in whatsoever state I am . . . to be content" (Philippians, 4:11, KJV).

On my seventieth birthday, my brother asked, "So what's different from when you turned sixty?"

I laughed. "Well, it takes me ten minutes longer to mow the lawn!"

Thirteen years later, my answer to Randy's question is, "Well, I can't do everything I once did. But I'm thankful for all I can do—including mowing the lawn with my 14" cordless electric mower."

. . .

Decades ago, my father taught me an important lesson. "Don't focus on how far you have to go, but on how far you have come." It serves me well. So does a favorite motto: Look to the future, but remember the past. It is pointless to mourn the good-or-not-so-good-old-days instead of living in the present.

God has given me a set of keys to unlock the door to contentment.

1. He is always in control. Governments falter, storms rage, disaster strikes, yet I need not fear. He asks me to trust Him in all circumstances;

2. He never leaves me or forsakes me, but is only a prayer away. No busy signals on the heavenly phone lines.

3. He has placed me where I can do the most good. What joy to see someone I have lent a helping hand go on to achieve a desired goal!

4. He leads me to those who need what I can offer. Sometimes it is only a smile in a grocery store. Or a chat with a neighbor. Yet each encounter blesses both me and the recipient.

5. He provides for all my needs. I will never be rich in the eyes of the world. Yet no amount of wealth can compare with the peace and love He sends.

6. He helps me recognize my limitations and not allow pride to stand in the way of admitting I sometimes need help. Example: Several weeks ago, I climbed a tall ladder to change a light bulb in the garage. Perched above the cement floor, I realized I shouldn't be there. I won't be again.

7. He sends helpers for tasks beyond my strength. Neighbors are there to perform tasks I no longer feel comfortable doing. (Everything from climbing on the roof and cleaning the gutters to changing light bulbs in the garage!)

8. He has given me a modest home in a cul-de-sac where I feel safe. People know and look out for me. Neighbors recently noticed I hadn't pulled the shades against the blazing afternoon sun. This was a deviation from my usual routine so they came over to make sure I was all right.

9. He reminds me to follow Dad's advice. When trouble comes, no asking, "Why me?" Instead, acceptance of things as they are, followed by, "Okay, God, where do we go from here?"

10. My life reflects words from the song, "He Leadeth Me."

"Lord, I would clasp Thy hand in mine, Nor ever murmur nor repine.

Content whatever lot I see, Since 'tis my God that

leadeth me."

"Thank You, Father, for Your endless love and care. In Jesus; name, Amen."

Colleen L. Reece learned to read by kerosene lamplight near her Darrington, WA home that was once a one-room schoolhouse where her mother taught all eight grades.

Love for God and family outweighed the lack of modern conveniences and became the basis for many of Colleen's books. Her "refuse to compromise" stance has won awards and praise from readers of many ages. One woman wrote, "Thank you for writing books I not only love but can hand to my twelve-going-on-eighteen-year-old-granddaughter without a qualm."

Colleen is best known for helping to launch Heartsong Presents Book Club in 1992 and was twice named Favorite Author in reader polls. In 1998, she and Tracie Peterson were the first authors inducted into the Heartsong Hall of Fame.

Life's Harbingers

By Peggy Blann Phifer

"To everything there is a season, a time for every purpose under heaven." Ecclesiastes 3:1-2 [NKJV]

The yard is full of robins. These birds are said to be the 'first harbingers of Spring,' always a welcome sight, letting us know that the long winter sleep is finally over.

But, at this time of year, they are telling me that it's time for their long migration south.

I'm also watching squirrels, gray, red … and an occasional rare black one … busily gathering and storing.

Bright yellow, red and orange leaves of the hardwood trees on our property, surround us with God's colorful artistry.

My son-in-law has put the lawn mower away, readied the snow blower, turned off the outside water, and moved things off the open deck, putting them where they'll be protected with an overhang.

Soon I'll be hearing honking geese flying down from the north in their V-formations, heading for warmer climes.

Harbingers*

Winter is on its way.

I must admit that this does not make me happy.

While I love the beauty of a pristine fresh snowfall, and the squeaky crunch of it beneath my feet as I walk, I hate the cold. And it doesn't like me. I suffer greatly in the winter, so I face the coming months with dread.

But isn't all this a lot like life in general? If you read the entire chapter of the scripture above, you'll see that the author of Ecclesiastes—presumably Solomon—goes on to list almost everything we face in our everyday walk through life at one time or another ... sometimes more than once.

1. Birth, death
2. Plant, harvest
3. Weep, laugh
4. Break down, build up
5. Mourn, dance
6. Gain, loss
7. Keep, throw away
8. Tear, sew
9. Speak, remain silent
10. Love, hate
11. War, peace

We ALL go through these seasons, like it or not. God ordained it that way. We need these seasons, good and bad, to grow. To strengthen us. To 'smarten us up' through trial and error. We try, and we fail. We try again. Maybe we fail again, so we try once more.

The thing is, we need to persevere. To keep trying, and believe God has a plan for us.

In Jeremiah 29:11, we see these words:

"For I know the thoughts that I think toward you, says the Lord, thoughts of peace and not of evil, to give you a future and a hope."

Back to Ecclesiastes Chapter three ... in verse 11, Solomon wrote: *"He has made everything beautiful in its time."*

Isn't that wonderful? No matter what we've gone through, *are* going through, and *will* go through in the future, God has something beautiful with which to reward us.

Even me, with my painful discomfort through what seem to be interminably long winter months, am forced to observe God's beauty all around me.

And that's a good thing.

Prayer: Lord God, thank you for your faithfulness to us. No matter the trials, no matter the pain or grief we face, You are always with us. Always there. Never failing. And for that we are grateful. Amen.

*Harbinger:
1: noun. Something that precedes and indicates the approach of something or someone
2: verb. Foreshadow or presage

Author Peggy Blann Phifer, a retired executive assistant after twenty-one years in the Electrical Wholesale Industry, lives in the 'boonies' of NW Wisconsin. A late bloomer, Peg didn't start taking writing seriously until age fifty.

Her debut novel, *To See the Sun,* a contemporary romantic suspense, released in January 2012. A second novel, *Somehow, Christmas Will Come,* contemporary women's fiction with a touch of romance, released in November 2014, revised and re-released in late 2015. Her work has also appeared in numerous anthologies, and she is currently working on an historical romantic suspense set during the years of Prohibition with a working title of *Whispering Hope.*

Peg is a member of American Christian Fiction Writers. When she's not writing, Peg enjoys reading, blogging, and sharing her home with her daughter, son-in-law, and a Border Collie mix dog named Rocky.

True Feminism

By Miriam Finesilver

The longing of my heart is to be protected (safe). There's something thrilling in experiencing a voluntary vulnerability, allowing myself to be touched, aware of my vulnerability yet choosing to trust. Being a true female, the way God created me to be. Touched and trusting. Warm, safe, and unguarded.

Ultimately it is accepting with joy the love of my Messiah. And in His love He made me a wife. My husband was given to me by God, yet Biblically I must say I was given to him—Abba presented me to my spouse. To really enjoy the gift Jesus gave me that I might experience true rest and my femininity blossoming—the delight of this sweet safe trust is received when I receive **God's authority**, and the man He chose to be authority over me in this life.

Thank you, Lord, for making me a woman. All the commands to walk with and abide in You, for me as a woman have become thrilling. This is TRUE FEMINISM.

Submission grants me the longing of my female heart, to be protected, because God is my loving, all wise Protector, King, Ruler and Husband.

Woman was presented to man and when she disobeyed her curse was to desire to master over her husband. It was a CURSE because it's a painful struggle, yet yielding to the purpose for which I was created is fulfilling.

1 Peter 3:3-4 New King James Version (NKJV)
3 Do not let your adornment be merely outward—arranging the hair, wearing gold, or putting on fine apparel— 4 rather let it be the hidden person of the heart, with the incorruptible beauty of a gentle and quiet spirit, which is very precious in the sight of God.

Always always it is about pleasing Him.

Miriam Finesilver lives in South Florida with her husband Michael. Together they speak at churches, present the Jewish Passover, equip Christians to share the Gospel with Jewish people, and a monthly newsletter. The author previously worked in New York City as an actress and playwright. You can visit her at miriamfinesilver.net

On Twitter, I have an account under Miriam Finesilver

On Facebook, it is MichaelandMimi Finesilver

I have a blog http://miriamfinesilver.net

Author's page on Amazon: https://www.amazon.com/Miriam-Finesilver/e/B00WT2QGNC

Seventeen Threads

By Linda Farmer Harris

Three hundred dollars?" Mrs. Reeves used my crisp white linen napkin to sop up the coffee sloshed out of her cup. "For a fourth grader's coat?"

"Of course. More coffee?" Didn't she understand it was a coup finding a one hundred percent camel hair coat in my daughter's diminutive size? When Maureen at Neiman-Marcus called, I didn't hesitate to authorize the purchase.

In May, 1978, my husband, Jerry, announced, "I want to be more than a Sunday-go-to-meetin' Christian. God is asking me to leave the ministry and teach in public schools. A rural environment will filter out all the distractions and get our family back on track."

Our city track was fine. Amanda attended a private school. I loved my work as a state agency sign language interpreter. I taught sign classes at the University of Texas and signed for two Dallas television programs. The only aggravation—Amanda would wear her new coat to the rural school.

We left our spacious five bedrooms, three and half baths, two-story brick home on Lake Benbrook for the sleepy farming community of Alvaredo, Texas, forty miles south of Fort Worth. The trade-off was dirt roads to a 900 sq. ft. fifty-year-old house with a barn and a catfish pond.

So, there I sat drinking coffee with a woman whose highest ambition in life was square dancing on Saturday nights at the VFW hall. She had a gaggle of noisy kids, in constant motion, and seldom tidy. The closest she came to make-up and nail polish was flour and food coloring.

I offered vanilla bean flavored sugar and real cream to a woman who stirred her home coffee with thin red plastic sticks from a convenience store.

In her own world of influence, she was incredible. Anyone who can recite detailed histories of fifteen major characters in four popular soap operas and never lose the story lines is amazing. Although, to her, GOP was short for gravy over potatoes, and the comic strip was the reason she read the newspaper. Yep, she was growing on me.

Jerry looked forward to services at the little church on the highway. No choir loft, organ, or padded benches, but Jesus Christ met them there when they prayed and worshiped.

My misery hit an all time high in December when some grimy-handed little urchin grabbed Amanda's coat from behind and ripped it.

Thankful the rip only separated the collar from the yoke, I gathered needle, thread, and scissors and detached the satin lining, which revealed a silk lining. I congratulated myself on a great purchase before I lifted away the third lining and flipped the coat inside out. I saw my life on the inside of a coat.

Jerry found me sitting in the middle of the kitchen floor clinging to a wad of coat and sobbing.

I pointed to the tear-soaked coat. "This is my spiritual graph."

He handed me his handkerchief. "All I see is a coat that needs to be repaired and dry cleaned."

"Black, magenta, blue, orange." I turned out one

sleeve then the other and pointed to more colors. "Seventeen different colors. I'm like this coat. Everything looks perfect on the outside, but I'm hiding behind satin and silk linings. I can't go on like this."

"What do you want to do?"

"I want to be like the song you've been singing all week, *Nothing Between My Soul and My Savior*."

Jerry gathered me into his arms. Tears streamed down his face. "I've been praying for this day for months. Last year God shook me every way but loose. I'd been playing Christian and flaunting it in the face of a Holy God. My greatest fear was that you would resist the changes." He pushed me back enough to look me in the eyes. "Maybe leave."

A pain clutched my heart in an anguish I'd never known before. In all my resistance to our new track, I'd never once considered leaving. Oh, what misery he endured.

He pulled me back into his arms. "I know the path God is asking us to walk is alien to everything we've ever known."

When I was overwhelmed and desperate, God alone knew which way I ought to turn. He used a song to guide my heart.

"Jerry, please start with the third verse—'Nothing between, like pride or station, self or friends shall not intervene; Tho' it may cost me much tribulation, I am resolved, there's nothing between.'"

The coat? Every stitch I plucked felt like God digging out my sins by the roots. I ripped every seam and sewed the coat together with one color of thread—red.

Red for the blood Jesus Christ shed for me on the cross when He paid the price for my sin against God. Red for my name written in the Lamb's Book of Life.

Mrs. Reeves? The Holy Spirit touched her heart. She

started a women's Bible Study in her home. The Time? During TV's afternoon prime time. She found something better than the soaps.

Me? I found a best friend, and a forever family track.

How about your heart? Is it right with God? Are you on the right track?

And they straightway left their nets, and followed him. Matthew 4:20

Linda (Lin) Farmer Harris and husband Jerry live in Northeast Oklahoma. Her passion for the Harvey Girls and the Southwestern Indian Detour Courier Corps; her travels in Mexico; plus her skills as a nationally certified interpreter for the deaf are included in her historical fiction for adult and middle graders.

When not writing or researching for her novels, Lin knits historical patterns. In honor of her father, a Merchant Marine and her brother, a Navy sailor, she knits the 1898 pattern for the scarf, beanie, and cowl for mariners through the volunteer program Christmas at Sea of The Seamen's Church Institute in Port Newark, New Jersey—http://seamenschurch.org/christmas-at-sea.

She creates and maintains websites for fellow writers and writers groups in Texas and Colorado. From 2013-2017, Lin wrote a monthly blog entry on the 27th for *Heroes, Heroines & History*—http://www.hhhistory.com.

Lin is a member of the American Christian Fiction Writers (ACFW); Wolf Creek Writers Network in Colorado; ACFW-Central Texas Chapter; Southwest Christian Writers Association, and ACFW-Colorado Western Slope Chapter.

Her novella, *Treasure Among the Ruins*, Book 1, Voices in the Desert Series, is available in Paperback & Kindle.

Her novella in the California Gold Rush Romance Collection, *The Lye Water Bride* starts on page 197 and is available in Paperback and Kindle.

Readers are welcomed to connect with Lin at http://www.lindafarmerharris.com or by email Linda@LindaFarmerHarris.com

Casting Our Child at The Lord's Feet

"Cast all your anxiety on Him because He cares for you." 1 Peter 5:7

E ach night as I climb into bed, I repeat the wise words in Philippians 4:8. As I prepare for another night where my mind attempts to capture me and hold me hostage, stealing my night's sleep, I focus on what is true, noble, right, pure, lovely, and admirable. Besides the Bible, I have read enough self-improvement books to know our life will follow what we focus on. The mind is most powerful. Each night it is like an intense battle as I also watch my daughter as she readies for bed, in a battle of her own against the demons of obsessive-compulsive disorder.

The multiple rituals she is compelled to perform before she can get into bed are draining and exhausting for her. As her mother, they are heart breaking and render me hopeless. As I watch her open and close the bathroom door, step out into the hall and step back into the bathroom, the panic begins. I go over the 'am I doing enough?' checklist in my mind, wondering if there isn't something I might not be doing to help her get well. She's in weekly therapy, takes a prescription with the least addictive possibilities, least side effects and so far, she has had no troubles. It's also still very new for her and we are watching to see when she will need to up her dosage.

Will she get on her feet? How will she function in the world? Will the medicine lessen the need to do her compulsions? What about her degree? Her dreams? Her goals? As I watch the movie in my mind, noble, right, pure, and lovely have been buried under a mountain of worries, fears and future what ifs.

For most of us, it is often a struggle to cast our care upon the Lord as the Bible instructs us to do. For a mother, it is even harder to cast our child at the Lord's feet, but I am trying. Each morning as I rise, I do so. Each night as I slip under the covers, I do so again. Like my daughter's battles, it is a constant ongoing struggle. But I hold on to hope, even in the darkest, most restless nights, that like the medicine that in time will diminish my daughter's compulsions, I will get better at casting my cares, my child, at the Lord's feet.

~ Christina Lorenzen

Christina Lorenzen started writing as a young teen, filling wire ring composition books with her imaginary worlds. Her first typewriter improved her speed of getting those stories out of her head and onto paper.

Her love of writing sustained her through a myriad of jobs including hairdresser, secretary, waitress and door to door saleswoman. Luckily for her, writing proved to be successful and a lot less walking than going door to door.

Christina writes sweet small-town romance. She is the author of seven books besides Howls & Hearts. She is busy working on her next small-town romance. When she isn't writing or reading, she can be found walking her dog, talking to her herd of cats and spending time with her grown children and husband.

To find out about Christina's upcoming release, visit her website at http://christinalorenzen.com. You can subscribe to her quarterly newsletter through her website and automatically be entered to win a $5 Amazon gift card each month, just for being a subscriber.

Waiting Expectantly

By Marilyn Turk

"In the morning, LORD, you hear my voice; in the morning I lay my requests before you and wait expectantly." Psalm 5:3 (NIV)

During my long sales career, I participated in many sales contests, motivated by the desire to win rewards. These rewards were monetary and were mailed to me sometime after the contest ended. As a result, I began to expect a check each time I received mail. With that in mind, my daily trip to the mailbox was exciting because I anticipated getting a reward.

That excited anticipation has remained with me ever since, long after my sales job ended. I still look forward to getting the mail, and sometimes I even get a check for something I've written.

In the same way, I expect God to answer my prayers. Psalm 5:3 echoes my feelings. Every day, I get up early in the morning to spend time with God. I pray, thanking God for what He has done and requesting him to do something else for me or for others. I know He hears me, so I wait for His answer, expecting it to come.

Of course, I know the answer might not always

be "yes." In fact, Dr. Charles Stanley says that God answers in three ways: "yes, no, and wait." Two out of three of those answers make me optimistic. In a world of instant gratification, waiting is sometimes the most difficult thing to do. But waiting is necessary to see the end result, even if the result is not in agreement with our own schedules. If God's answer to me seems delayed, that doesn't mean He said "no." It could mean He said, "Not yet." And if He said that, I can continue to wait and expect to see the answer.

And quite possibly, that answer can arrive in the mail!

Lord, thank you for hearing my prayers. Please help me to wait while I expect your answer.

Who am I?

By Marilyn Turk

"For you created my inmost being; you knit me together in my mother's womb. I praise you because I am fearfully and wonderfully made; your works are wonderful, I know that full well. My frame was not hidden from you when I was made in the secret place, when I was woven together in the depths of the earth. Your eyes saw my unformed body; all the days ordained for me were written in your book before one of them came to be." Psalm 139:13-16

I attend a large women's Bible study at our church, one where it's impossible to know everyone, no matter how hard you try.

While standing in line for the restroom, the woman in front of me turned around and studied my name tag. "You're the writer." It didn't sound like a question, but I answered anyway. "Yes, I am an author." At that moment, someone else spoke to her and diverted her attention, so our conversation ended.

Later, as I pondered the interaction, I thought about how my identity had changed over the years. From child to student to single career woman to wife to mother to grandmother. I'm a sister, a cousin, an aunt and an in-law. I've been a team mom, VBS teacher and scout leader. Other titles

I've had were office clerk, newspaper layout artist, television research sales assistant, magazine receptionist, salesperson, sales manager, product specialist, major account manager. I've been a Sunday School teacher, a choir member, a Bible study facilitator, bazaar bake sale coordinator, seminar host and conference director.

Thankfully, I didn't hold all those titles at once. These labels described who I was because of what I've done. But who am I really? I guess the only one who can answer that is God. Because as Psalm 139 says, He created me and He knows how long I'll live.

Most importantly, I'm a child of God. As Galatians 3: 26 says, "So in Christ Jesus you are all children of God through faith."

And that identity trumps the rest.

Lord, thank you for knowing me for who I really am and loving me so much you allowed me to become your child through faith in your Son Jesus.

Marilyn Turk Bio

Historical fiction flavored with suspense and romance

Multi-published author Marilyn Turk calls herself a "literary archaeologist," because she loves to discover stories hidden in history. Her World War II novel, *The Gilded Curse*, won a Silver Scroll award. When readers asked what happened to the characters after the book, Marilyn wrote the sequel, *Shadowed by a Spy*. Her four-book Coastal Lights Legacy series—Rebel Light, Revealing Light, Redeeming Light, and Rekindled Light—feature Florida lighthouse settings. In addition, Marilyn's novella, *The Wrong Survivor,* is in the Gre*at Lakes Lighthouse Brides* collection. Marilyn has also written a book of devotions called *Lighthouse Devotions*. Marilyn writes for the *Daily Guideposts Devotions* book.

She is a regular contributor to the Heroes, Heroines and History blog, (https://www.hhhistory.com) as well as the Christians Read blog, (https://christiansread.wordpress.com).

Marilyn is also the director of the Blue Lake Christian Writers Retreat. http://bluelakecwr.com.

She lives in the panhandle of Florida where she and her husband enjoy boating, fishing, and playing tennis when time permits (and it's below 100 degrees).

Website: @http://pathwayheart.com
Email: marilynturkwriter@yahoo.com

[i] James 5:17,18 NIV
[ii] Matthew 21:22 NIV
[iii] I Kings 17-19 NIV
[iv] John 17:20 NIV
[v] James 5:16b NIV
[vi] I Thessalonians 5:16-17 NIV
[vii] I John 1:9 NIV
[viii] Hebrews 4:16 NIV
[ix] James 5:19NIV
[x] James 1:6 NIV
[xi] C.S. Lewis. *Letters to Malcolm: Chiefly on Prayer*, Harvest Books, 1964.

Made in the USA
Columbia, SC
09 November 2018